As Day Dawns

inspiration for a busy life

A Lion Book
an imprint of
Lion Hudson plc
Mayfield House, 256 Banbury Road,
Oxford OX2 7DH, England
www.lionhudson.com
ISBN 978 0 7459 5207 9
ISBN 0 7459 5207 0

First edition 2006
10 9 8 7 6 5 4 3 2 1 0

Picture acknowledgments
pp. 2–3, 13, 30–31, 36, 50–51, 55, 62–63, 66, 77, 110–111 copyright © Geoff Nobes.
pp. 7, 68–69, 72–73, 86–87, 97, 118–119, 122, 126–127 copyright © Digital Vision.
pp. 17, 32–33, 107, 114–115 copyright © Punchstock.
pp. 20–21, 28, 41, 43, 59, 92, 102, 105 copyright © Getty Images.
pp. 48–49, 81 copyright © Alamy Ltd.
pp. 88–89 copyright © Jonathan Roberts.

A catalogue record for this book is available
from the British Library

Typeset in 9/12 Americana BT
Printed and bound in China

As Day Dawns

inspiration for a busy life

Helen Jaeger

To my friends. Let us be
all we are capable of being.

Contents

Introduction

Each day is a gift. This may sound like a trite phrase, but I believe it to be true. That said, I freely admit that the snooze button on my alarm clock is the most overused piece of technology in my house.

I would really love to be one of those people who rises with the lark to see in the first rosy streaks of dawn as they steal across the eastern horizon. I'd like to say I'm familiar with the cool, clean air with which mornings, even in cities, reward the early riser. I'd like, even, to be on first-name terms with the person who delivers my post or takes away my rubbish. I'd like to... but I'm not.

So how can I say that each day is a gift? If I truly believe this, shouldn't it have me leaping out of bed, fresh with renewed vigour and trilling, 'Morning has broken'?

Well, yes and no. Each day is a gift, at whatever time of day we begin to live that gift. What marks us out as life-appreciators is more the attitude that carries us through the day than the hour at which we rise.

Several centuries before we arrived on the scene, a man called Benedict from northern Italy was asking a very important question about attitudes: 'What does it mean to live out good news in *my* times?' For Benedict, this good news was the news of God's love, and having pondered this question for a number of years, he eventually wrote the Rule of Benedict, which shaped a way of living and founded a now thriving system of spirituality and community throughout the world.

So what has Benedict got to do with you or me getting out of bed?

Reflecting on Benedict's question as we begin our daily round can be a source of great inspiration. What does it mean to live out this good news in *our* times, when we wake up to a world blown up by terrorists, engulfed by tsunamis, flattened by hurricanes, afflicted

by incurable diseases and ground down by poverty and war? What does it mean to apply the inspiration of the good news to our personal lives, the circumstances of which may include hardship or suffering? I'm no Benedict, but I do have certain beliefs and they go something like this...

First and foremost, I believe living out the good news means understanding with our whole beings that we are **loved** by the divine and that every day is an **adventure** further into this love.

I believe working and resting in the divine blessing means routinely experiencing robust **hope** and tender **compassion** – not as something that we manufacture, but as something we receive.

I believe the divine wants to inspire us in **receiving**

the opportunities that life offers, and invites us to ground such activity in wholesome **reflection**.

I believe that entering into the care of the divine – whether we work or rest – gives rise to a capacity for infinite **wonder** in the place of a fashionable and prevalent cynicism, and that such an attitude of wonder can lead us to the thresholds of **beauty**, where our souls are fed and freed.

I believe this means we will delight in **joy**, whatever the circumstances of our lives, and that this joy is part of the **mystery** of life, which we are all invited to savour.

I believe living out the good news means discovering and valuing **home**, even as we adventure and **work** all over the globe.

I believe we are invited to a life of revolutionary **gentleness**, in which we resist the shattering forces of violence, fear and revenge, and instead we work for **justice** and **peace** for all.

Finally, I believe that living out the good news means that we will be broken and blessed, but that we then become **gifts ourselves**, given to the world by a divine and kind hand.

Suggested ways to use this book

This book is divided into fifteen inspirational paths, covering some of the ground to which I've alluded above. Each path has an introductory comment, a Bible passage with questions, an imaginative meditation, a prayer, a poem and a range of quotes about the subject from mostly well-known authors. You should not feel obliged to work through each path in one go or even sequentially. Pick and choose what seems most appropriate to you at any time and, if you like, carry it with you through your day.

Introduction

This is a short section designed to help you begin to think about each particular path. It introduces key features you may like to consider and is drawn from personal experience – although, truth be told, some of what I have written is a little like a blueprint or strategy for paths I want to explore in more depth myself, and in this way I become your fellow adventurer, too.

Meditation

Each Bible passage has been chosen for its relevance to the path in question. I suggest you read the passage slowly, allowing any words or thoughts from it to hold your attention. You may like to repeat words or phrases to yourself, allowing them to sink fully into your mind and heart. Do not rush this. Allow the passage to speak to you and your personal situation.

When you feel you have gleaned all possible nourishment from the Bible passage, you may like to move on to the questions attached to it. Use the questions as a way of turning over the Bible passage in your mind and entering into its truths more fully. If the questions don't appeal to you, skip them. But if there are particular questions that arrest your attention, make a response to them in whatever way is most suitable for you (for example, in a journal or prayer) or consider them throughout your day.

Imagine

I suggest you read through the imaginative meditation before you do it, so you have a good idea of what you are going to be contemplating. When you are ready, close your eyes and use the meditation as a basis for exploring each path more creatively.

Each meditation also has a few questions attached to it. Again, these are designed to help not to hinder you. You don't have to have an immediate answer to the question, but it may be something you want to return to in subsequent days, allowing answers and wisdom to come from the deep places within you.

Prayer

Each path has its own short prayer. Speaking others' prayers is effective – particularly if you are in a rush in the morning. If you wish to pray your own prayers, remember that you can express yourself however you wish.

Poem

The poems in this book are another way for you to enter into each path more intuitively. Each poem is written from personal experience and, again, reflects an aspect of the theme. You may like to read the poems slowly and carefully, reflecting on their message to you. In this way, you may find truth comes to you through symbol and metaphor. You could also respond in your own innovative way to the poems, exploring their significance more personally.

Inspirations

The quotes in each path have not been selected at random, but have been chosen to fit with the theme. Some quotes grab us and sum up what we are thinking and feeling at any one time. This is the power of words. Allow the words of others to inspire and encourage you. You may like to stick relevant quotes around your home and workspace.

Finally

We may find that the divine mixes up our lives a little – we may be called to a gentle hope or invited into the mystery of love. We may experience a peaceful joy or an adventure into compassion. What struck me as I wrote this book is just how many of these attitudes overlap and interweave. Perhaps at the end of your reading you may want to reflect on your own unique attitudes to your path of life. Perhaps you will want to ask for yourself: 'What does it mean to live out the good news in my times?' I hope that what you discover here will inspire you, enrich you and strengthen you, as your day dawns – whatever time of day that happens to be.

Love notes

I was reading a novel in which each of the central characters receives a secret message inside an envelope with their name written on it. The message in the envelope is always one of great foreboding, creating a sense of anxiety in each character. But it got me thinking: if each of us were to receive a secret message today, perhaps even a message from the divine, what would that message say?

Maybe the message would be simple. Maybe the message would be just three words: I love you. I think this because I believe all our lives are about this very thing – coming into our own unique belovedness. Yes, all our lives are about becoming who we really are, the person the divine imagination saw us to be before the birth even of the stars.

All our lives are a journey into understanding that we are loved. This is the truth and this is love. Of course, we hear other messages: 'You're not good enough; you're useless; you don't measure up.' Sometimes we try to live by those messages. We choose a lie over the truth, frequently because we don't know any better. And so our lives produce the fruit of such misunderstanding: failure, broken relationships, low self-esteem, division.

But this is not the truth. The reality is that we are deeply, compassionately loved. Realizing this sets us free, not merely in a physical sense, but in a psychological sense, too. And so, sooner or later, we try to live, even if tentatively, out of our belovedness.

How that looks may be different for each one of us. For me, the revelation that I was deeply loved came slowly, and with it came a slow freedom, amazement and a great joy. I began to live more boldly, understanding for the first time that all of me is embraced by all of the divine: my faults embraced by compassion; my strengths embraced with joy and celebration.

As I trusted more and could bring all of myself to all

of the divine, I began to feel safe. I felt peace, profound peace. No longer did I need to run, to hide, to protect myself. I found that the divine gaze is, at its essence, the gaze of the lover on the beloved. Even my fiery passion was embraced by gentle love.

Furthermore, I learned that what was broken in me, what caused me frustration, could be healed. The nervous energy in me became calmed, not so that I lost my zeal, but so that I could be safely held. I discovered that we are loved, we are held, we are cherished.

In this way we are all becoming beloved, living up to our first calling, which is to be the treasured children of the divine. Our life is a journey into love and love is our destination. This is what I discovered, and while parts of

me hardly dared to believe it, the adventurous, courageous part of me began to rejoice in the journey itself. I didn't need to prove myself. I could simply be, in all my brokenness and all my wholeness. Love never lets us go.

So how do messages of this love come to us? This is how they come to me: in dreams, in daydreams, in books, in films, in song lyrics, in art, in the breathtakingly beautiful enchantment of creation, in the touch and care of friends and family, in the innocent eyes of a child, in silence, in communion. The channels are endless.

The world will try to whisper all kinds of lies to us today. It may try to tell us that we are not loved, that love is a myth, that we must take love piecemeal and in scrappy fashion, wherever and whenever it's offered. But this, too, is not true. True love perseveres, shelters, delights, hears, sympathizes – even challenges, when the challenge is to be our better selves. And I realized, too, that the divine falls in love with us, asking nothing, desiring everything. The divine is always the greater lover in this way.

I do not write about this great love as a stranger to hardship, grief or stress. I live in the thick of the world, as we all do. And I cannot say with all truthfulness that I live up to my vocation every day. I cannot say that I understand what it means to know that the divine is in love with me (and with you) every day, but I have a new sense that the invitation is there. And *that's* what I want to explore. That's what I want to live by. In all the inevitable challenges of the day, as well as all the joy, I want to learn what it means to be a witness to love, for this is my calling and, perhaps, it is yours too.

Meditation

Read

For God so loved the world that he gave his only Son, that whoever believes in him should not perish but have eternal life. For God did not send his Son into the world to condemn the world, but in order that the world might be saved through him.

John 3:16–17

Beloved, let us love one another, because love is from God; everyone who loves is born of God and knows God.

1 John 4:7

He said, 'Do not fear, greatly beloved, you are safe. Be strong and courageous!'

Daniel 10:19

Consider

Think of a time when you have experienced love from other people. How did that feel? Can you see the divine being expressed to you in this way by other people? Would you like to grow in the expression of genuine care to others?

Can you believe that you belong to the divine through a bond of love, and that through that same bond the divine belongs to you?

Perhaps you experience other emotions when you encounter the divine presence. Perhaps, like Daniel, you feel fear or awe. But within those emotions, can you hear the word of love which is addressed to you today?

Imagine

Imagine that you receive a gold envelope in the post today. On it is written your name and also the words 'personal and confidential'. On the back is a heavy wax seal of your favourite symbol. You have no idea what is in the envelope, but it feels heavy and is obviously made of good quality paper. Suddenly you notice some instructions written in italic on the back of the envelope. They say, 'To be opened in private and not to be seen by anyone else.' You choose when and where you are going to open the envelope – maybe you can do it straight away or maybe you will choose a special time later in the day.

When the time comes, you carefully undo the envelope. Inside is one sheet of heavyweight paper in your favourite colour with an imprint of your favourite image on it. Whoever has sent you this letter clearly knows you very well. You read the message on the paper. It is a message that communicates great love and understanding to you. Slowly you begin to smile.

Go through this meditation slowly, noticing how you feel at each stage and how you reacted to the envelope. Were you nervous, excited, cynical, curious? Think about why you chose to open the envelope in the way you did – what does it tell you about yourself? Now imagine what that message said. Maybe it was a message of love or of hope, or a promise of security or protection or adventure...? What does that message tell you about your life right now? What message of love might the divine be trying to communicate with you today and what difference might it make to you to take that message to heart?

Prayer

God of love, you speak in lover's notes to me every day. Help me to see, hear and notice your love around me. Open my eyes, mind, heart and spirit to your great love. I offer my entire self to you, no holds barred, for you are both my lover and my friend. Amen.

Poem

This new old news

And so I asked the divine
To write this new
Old news on my heart:

'Write that I am loved,' I said,
'For I will easily forget.

'This world will pull me
In many different directions,
But your love is both an anchor and a sail.

'With you, I am on safe ground and
With you, I can journey safely on.'

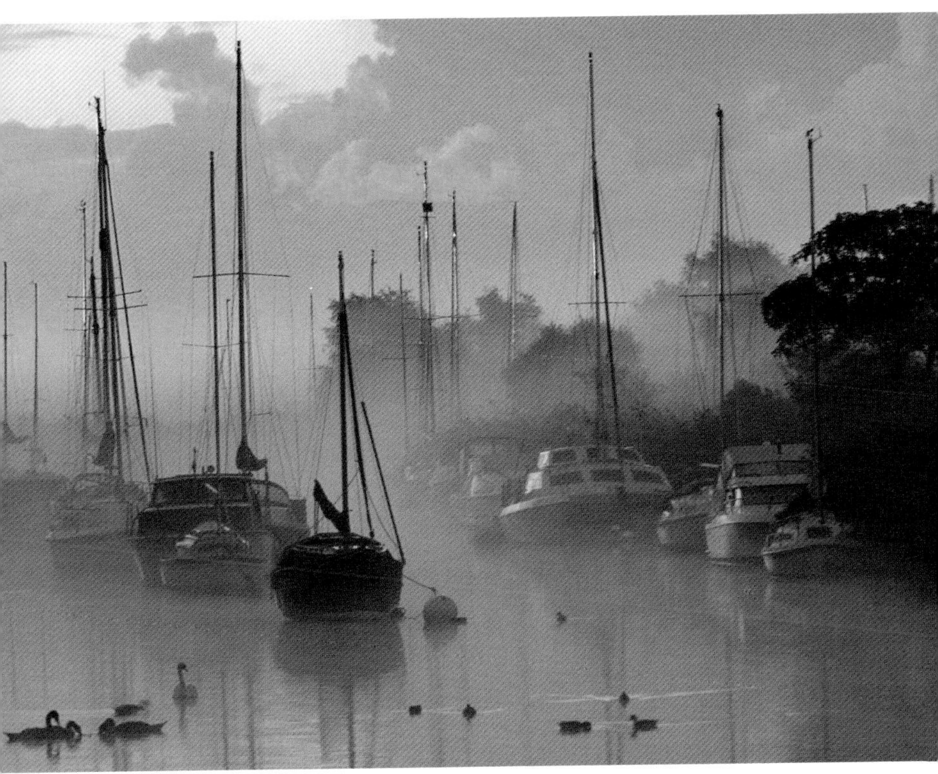

Inspirations

Life has taught us that love does not consist in gazing at each other but in looking outward together in the same direction.

Antoine de Saint-Exupéry

My debt to you, Beloved,
Is one I cannot pay
In any coin of any realm
On any reckoning day.

Jessie B. Rittenhouse

Love is, above all, the gift of oneself.

Jean Anouilh

Love never reasons but profusely gives; gives, like a thoughtless prodigal, its all, and trembles lest it has done too little.

Hannah Moore

Love is not love which alters when it alteration finds.

William Shakespeare

The way to love anything is to realize that it may be lost.

G. K. Chesterton

There's nothing more freeing than the shackles of love.

Emma Racine de Fleur

Love is the greatest refreshment in life.

Pablo Picasso

Just because someone doesn't love you the way you want them to, doesn't mean they don't love you with all they have.

Anonymous

Come live in my heart and pay no rent.

Samuel Lover

Love is to let those we love be perfectly themselves and not to twist them to fit our own image, otherwise we love only the reflection of ourselves we find in them.

Anonymous

I need the starshine of your heavenly eyes
After the day's great sun.

Charles Hanson Towne

The sustaining power of the Beloved Presence has through the ages made the sickbed sweet and the graveside triumphant; transformed broken hearts and relations; brought glory to drudgery, poverty and old age; and turned the martyr's stake or noose into a place of coronation.

Dallas Willard

He is my Altar, I His holy place; I am His guest, and He my living food; I'm His by penitence, He is mine by grace; I'm His by purchase, He is mine by blood; He's my supporting elm, and I His vine: Thus I my Best-beloved's am; thus He is mine.

Francis Quarles

It is a serious thing to live in a society of possible gods and goddesses, to remember that the dullest and most uninteresting person you talk to may one day be a creature which, if you saw it now, you would be strongly tempted to worship – or else a horror and a corruption such as you now meet, if at all, only in a nightmare. All day long we are, in some degree, helping each other to one or other of these destinations. It is in the light of these overwhelming possibilities, it is with the awe and the circumspection proper to them, that we should conduct all our dealings with one another, all friendships, all loves, all play, all politics. There are no ordinary people.

C. S. Lewis

Enjoy the adventure

I grew up in a town in the East Midlands, and at the age of eighteen I had spent all of my life in the same place. I knew how to get from one place to another without needing road names. Shortcuts I had once walked with my Dad as a child became circuits for bike racing with my friends and, later still, I ditched the bike for a car that I could drive down the streets, roads and avenues that I knew so well.

My best friend lived at the other end of town. Throughout our childhood and teenage lives, we swam in the same town pool and walked through the same park where we had played tag, caught fish in the brook and collected bagfuls of autumn conkers.

But by the age of eighteen I was more than ready to leave. I believed I knew it all and could do it all. So I bought a rucksack and a Europe-wide train ticket with the money I'd earned doing a night-time shelf-stacking job at the local supermarket. Then I set off from the old Victorian station, which was a fifteen-minute walk from home. I went across Europe (twice), stayed in Israel and strayed into Egypt, where a memorable crescent moon upended directly over my head.

One hot evening eleven months later, surrounded by the Arabic architecture of Granada, I finally decided I had had enough of living out of a rucksack. Foregoing the rumoured splendour of Seville's Cathedral, I boarded a Spanish train and headed home. But my wanderlust didn't quite end there. I still made it out to India, the Middle East and Africa again. My travelling was a mix of grand adventure, mundane reality and a lot of mosquito bites. But whatever the pains and pleasures, I wouldn't have missed it for anything.

Yet it's worth remembering that we don't have to go far to be able to adventure. Every journey is an adventure, however modest. No one has walked down

the same stretch of street at exactly the same time and in exactly the same way as you are walking down it. The mix of what will happen is totally unique. Isn't that a wonder? When I grow weary of routine, I remember to approach life as a traveller. In this way, I come to every event and every person, however familiar or unfamiliar, with the eyes of innocence and discovery. That's adventure, too.

I have come to realize this: we are not called to know everything and to have experienced everything. One of the great joys, one of the great attitudes we can take into our day is that of the adventurer. This year, this day, will not come again. What are we to make of it? What will it make of us? Taking this approach to our day, however ordinary we anticipate it to be, makes for zest in place of weary jadedness. Life is a journey and its interest is not simply in the destination, but in how we get there and who we become along the way.

Meditation

Read

The man gazed at her in silence to learn whether or not the Lord had made his journey successful.

Genesis 24:21

The angel of the Lord came a second time, touched him, and said, 'Get up and eat, otherwise the journey will be too much for you.'

1 Kings 19:7

So they resumed their journey, putting the little ones, the livestock, and the goods in front of them.

Judges 18:21

Consider

Can you believe that your adventuring may be divinely inspired and that the divine cares about its outcome? What would you define as a successful journey?

Can you believe that your strength and stamina are issues of concern to the divine? How can you show the same care to others that the divine shows to you in your journey through life today?

So often we try to journey quickly. We are impatient with those who are slow – for example, the elderly and the very young. How might it change your journeying today to have regard for those who are weaker or slower? Could it be a blessing to you to do so?

Imagine

Imagine a conversation between a great traveller and a younger traveller. They are seated together in the great traveller's study in comfortable, leather armchairs before a roaring fire. On the walls are many photographs and pictures showing places the great traveller has visited or expeditions he/she has led. One wall of the study is entirely covered in bookshelves, containing books, travel guides and maps. There are a few curios around the room gathered from far-flung corners of the globe. Allow your eyes to rove around the room, taking in all the details. Now turn your attention to the two figures seated before the fire. They are in the middle of a fascinating conversation. The great traveller wants to pass on wisdom and advice to the young apprentice. What might you overhear in the conversation? The younger traveller wants to ask questions of the experienced traveller. What kinds of questions might be asked? You listen for a while, taking note of what is said.

When you imagined this scene, what in particular did you notice around the great traveller's room? What were you particularly drawn to (for example, maps, photos, particular travel books, artefacts from certain countries)? What might this tell you about your own inner desires for adventure? Do you see your desires in a literal sense (do you want to travel to a particular country) or in a symbolic sense (were you drawn to photos depicting great mountains because you want a new challenge)? Allow yourself time to mull over the details and possible reasons for those details.

Now recall the conversation between the great traveller and the younger traveller. Did you relate more to the experienced traveller or to the younger traveller? What did you learn from their conversation? Can you imagine the divine as the great traveller who is willing to pass on information to you as you journey through life? What might you like to ask the divine adventurer about today?

Prayer

God of freedom, you watch our comings and goings with interest and care. You it is who makes us adventure and you who keeps tender vigilance over our adventuring. I want to journey today. Be with me. Make me your prisoner, great king of freedom, that I may journey freely and safely throughout your world. Amen.

Poem

Goings on

Feel it
Here, in your heart.

Look,
I'll put my strong hand
On you
And pronounce a blessing.

Hear my words
Like the sharp, cool whisper of the wind:

The adventure
Is only just

Beginning.

Inspirations

Life is either a daring adventure or nothing. Security does not exist in nature, nor do the children of men as a whole experience it. Avoiding danger is no safer in the long run than exposure.

Helen Keller

Life ought to be a struggle of desire toward adventures whose nobility will fertilize the soul.

Rebecca West

Knowledge is an unending adventure at the edge of uncertainty.

Jacob Bronowski

The conquest of fear yields the courage of life. That is the cardinal initiation of every heroic adventure – fearlessness and achievement.

Joseph Campbell

Never forget that life can only be nobly inspired and rightly lived if you take it bravely and gallantly, as a splendid adventure in which you are setting out into an anonymous country, to meet many a joy, to find many a comrade, to win and lose many a battle.

Annie Besant

We love because it's the only true adventure.

William Gladstone

The worship of God is not a rule of safety: it is an adventure of the spirit, a flight after the unattainable. The death of religion comes with the repression of the high hope of adventure.

Alfred North Whitehead

Adventure is not outside a man; it is within.

David Grayson

We live in a wonderful world that is full of beauty, charm and adventure. There is no end to the adventures that we can have if only we seek them with our eyes open.

Jawaharlal Nehru

An adventure is only an inconvenience rightly considered. An inconvenience is only an adventure wrongly considered.

G. K. Chesterton

It is only in adventure that some people succeed in knowing themselves – in finding themselves.

André Gide

We are each gifted in a unique and important way. It is our privilege and our adventure to discover our own special light.

Mary Dunbar

A small, defiant hope

Rosa Parks was exhausted. She'd had a long, tiring day at work. Her feet ached – no, her whole body ached. She just wanted to get home. Most of us know how that feels. So Rosa Parks boarded the bus. Finding an empty seat, she slumped wearily into it. She thought it would be a tiring, crowded, uneventful journey home. But the next thing she knew, a gentleman was staring angrily down at her.

He demanded that she get up – this bone-tired, fragile woman – and give him her seat. Rosa Parks looked up at him and something inside her said 'no'. Then something outside her – her voice – said 'no', too. For Rosa Parks' act of supposed defiance, her refusal to give up her bus seat, she was prosecuted and sentenced to prison. This was America in 1968.

Sometimes I think we see hope as something brave, strong and positive. We have no problem seeing it in the face of the zealous placard-waver or in the courageous stand of the whistle-blower. We see hope flourish when the unjustly imprisoned man becomes a world leader, when concrete walls that divide people come tumbling down, when dictatorships and wars end.

But I see it, too, in the figure of a frail, black woman who refused to say 'yes', simply because she was too tired. Rosa Parks may not have felt hopeful as she stared up into the angry eyes of her white fellow-passenger. She may not have felt hopeful as she said 'no', and was subsequently imprisoned. Yet her single act of defiance became a symbol of hope and courage for oppressed black Americans everywhere.

Hope is often defiant. Our world does not always want change. Sometimes we may feel as though the world is laughing at our attempts to imagine and to bring about anything other than what is. Yet hope does not always have to be bold and make headlines to be true. Slumping down where we are, as Rosa Parks did, refusing to be moved, may be part of the politics of hope. So may many of the quiet, courageous, unseen acts that occur in our homes, families, workplaces and communities. Hope is not always strong. On the contrary, it can feel like a small, trembling, fragile thing. It can feel like a huge risk – which it is, because when we hope, we go out on a limb. We say that we believe that something, as yet unseen, may still emerge. The rhetoric of hope, like hope itself, is often tentative in this way, yet tentative is not the opposite of brave.

Yes, there is a place for the bold and the brave; but so, too, there is a place for a small, sheltered hope. There is a place for a whisper of hope. There is a place for a frail hope. Small and weary we may be. But if we can stay hopeful today, we are all potential world-changers.

Meditation

Read

And you will have confidence, because there is hope; you will be protected and take your rest in safety.

Job 11:18

Our soul waits for the Lord; he is our help and shield. Our heart is glad in him, because we trust in his holy name. Let your steadfast love, O Lord, be upon us, even as we hope in you.

Psalm 33:20–22

For surely I know the plans I have for you, says the Lord, plans for your welfare and not for harm, to give you a future with hope.

Jeremiah 29:11

Hope does not disappoint us, because God has poured out his love into our hearts by the Holy Spirit, whom he has given us.

Romans 5:5

Consider

What are your hopes for today? Are they for confidence or protection or rest or safety? For success or wisdom or

insight or care? Name your hopes.

Who or what are you hoping in today? Have you placed your hopes in a person who is able to deliver them? Or has someone set their hopes on you? What would it mean to put your hope in the divine – what strength or help might you be calling on to do so?

However good or challenging the situation in your own life today, can you believe the divine has a grand plan for you? Can you believe that plan is precisely about your welfare and your future? If you really believed this, what effect might it have on your attitude to the day?

Perhaps you have hoped but have been disappointed. Can you bring that disappointment now to the divine? Can you ask for the hope that you need?

Imagine

Imagine a high tree in a garden. It is almost dusk. The last of the sun's rays spread across the tree, bathing its branches in a gentle, golden light. Suddenly you notice a blackbird alight on the topmost bough of the tree. He is proud and glossy in his plumage. He opens his beak to sing. You decide to be still and to listen. The blackbird sings a glorious song, which fills your heart with delight.

Now imagine that tree is your heart. The blackbird's melody is a message which the divine wants to express

from your heart. Can you be still and listen? Can you delight in the song that you are hearing in your heart right now? What name might you give that song? Perhaps the divine wants to compose a song of hope from your heart for you and others to hear. If you face a challenging, stressful or uncertain day, how could you carry the memory of that melody into those situations?

Prayer

God of hope, I come to you with deep trust, hope and thanksgiving in my heart. As deep as any hardship, doubt or uncertainty goes, so your grace goes deeper. Sing your song of hope in me and through me today. Give me confidence. Help me to believe in the good that is not yet seen, but which may yet come to be. Amen.

Poem

Glimmers

That day we stood
On the summit of a hill
And watched the world.

Light leapt dim land,
Slipped shadows from fields,
Chased blackness
Across the ruffled lake.

Child, I've come to tell you
One thing, one thing
I learnt that day:

Hope can flash
Through the darkest place,
Sudden

Like a bright bird,

Like a bright bird
Upon the wing.

Inspirations

Once you choose hope,
anything's possible.
Christopher Reeve

When the world says, 'Give up,'
Hope whispers, 'Try it one more
time.'
Anonymous

Hope begins in the dark, the
stubborn hope that if you just
show up and try to do the right
thing, the dawn will come.
Anne Lamott

Hope is patience with the lamp lit.
Tertullian

Hope is faith holding out its hand
in the dark.
George Iles

And sanguine hope through every storm of life,
Shoots her bright beams, and calms the internal strife.
William Watson

Hope is putting faith to work when doubting would be
easier.
Anonymous

Hope is the word which God has written on the brow of
every man.
Victor Hugo

When you say a situation or a person is hopeless, you're
slamming the door in the face of God.
Charles L. Allen

Hope is the thing with feathers
That perches in the soul,
And sings the tune without the words,
And never stops at all,
And sweetest in the gale is heard;
And sore must be the storm
That could abash the little bird
That kept so many warm.
I've heard it in the chillest land,
And on the strangest sea;
Yet, never, in extremity,
It asked a crumb of me.

Emily Dickinson

Hope never abandons you. You abandon it.

George Weinberg

Hope is but the dream of those that wake.

Matthew Prior

Prosperity is not without many fears and distastes, and adversity is not without comforts and hopes.

Francis Bacon

To-day is not yesterday: we ourselves change; how can our Works and Thoughts, if they are always to be the fittest, continue always the same? Change, indeed, is painful; yet ever needful; and if Memory have its force and worth, so also has Hope.

Thomas Carlyle

Know then, whatever cheerful and serene
Supports the mind, supports the body too:
Hence, the most vital movement mortals feel
Is hope, the balm and lifeblood of the soul.

John Armstrong

In the midst of winter, I found there was, within me, an invincible summer.

Albert Camus

Compassionate tears

I was listening for the first time to a track on a new CD, while writing another chapter of this book. Suddenly, certain unfamiliar lyrics grabbed me and without any warning, I burst into tears. I stopped to wonder what this potent fusion of words, music and emotion had been about.

I thought of a friend in the throes of a mental illness; then of another, who had endured the stress and heartache of several failed IVF attempts. My mind turned to a different friend, struggling with debt, and to still another who, burnt out by a job that had promised so much yet demanded even more, was now doubtful about her own giftedness and vocation. Tears spilled out of me again.

But I knew inside myself that these flowing tears were not for me. I was not crying because the lyrics of the song were expressing something on my own heart. This feeling was different. Something was being put into me, not taken out. The divine had grabbed me and was unexpectedly at work. And if that was the case, what was going on? Was it perhaps, I wondered tentatively, about compassion?

I used to be a big fan of compassion, if 'fan' is the right word. Even when I was little, I knew I wanted somehow to work with people who were impoverished, and for a long time this was a guiding principle in my life – all through school, college and work. I didn't believe anyone was beyond the pale. Some of my best friends were people who had suffered much in their lives and had experienced a kind of poverty. My heart was deeply involved with them. But somewhere along the line, my compassion grew weary.

I saw people being taken advantage of, used and manipulated. I heard the cynicism of those who had worked for a long time trying to alleviate suffering and who now felt that their efforts were at best limited, and at worst a waste of time. I saw so much suffering in the world that I forgot to look at its beauty.

That night I had been listening to the current international number one album. And in doing so, I realized that there was something else I needed to understand about compassion. I saw afresh that compassion is not limited. I realized that compassion isn't restricted to any in-crowd or held back by physical walls in physical places. It cannot be exhausted: the merciful divine stands waiting to embrace all of us with love and tenderness, and to accept us just as we are. I felt with conviction that the divine does not simply dole out compassion in a meagre fashion to those who earn it. Instead it is poured out on all of our heads, at all times and in all places. In this way, maybe, compassion comes to us and through us.

The only way I can describe the compassion I

experienced that evening is that it was as if a great roaring river rushed through me. Maybe this powerful surge was clearing out some of my own preconceptions and judgments, cleaving a new, straight, clean path through my own heart? I didn't know and I don't yet know why. Only the days to come will tell. All I can say, with conviction, is that compassion is a truly holy thing.

Meditation

Read

Some had to bear being pilloried and flogged or even chained up in prison. They were stoned, or sawn in half, or killed by the sword; they were homeless, and wore only the skins of sheep and goats; they were in want and hardship and maltreated. They were too good for the world and they wandered in deserts and mountains and in caves and ravines.

Hebrews 11:36–38

The Lord is gracious and merciful, slow to anger and abounding in steadfast love. The Lord is good to all, and his compassion is over all that he has made.

Psalm 145:8–9

Can a woman forget her sucking child, that she should have no compassion on the son of her womb? Even these may forget, yet I will not forget you.

Isaiah 49:15

Consider

How much are the judgments you make about people based on what you see of their outward appearance? How might compassion change the way you view others? Can you agree with the writer of Hebrews that people who may apparently have very difficult lives may in reality be 'too good for the world'?

Can you believe that the divine has compassion over everyone at all times?

Can you believe that the divine's compassion is greater than that of a mother for a son she loves very much? Would you like to know this compassion for yourself?

Imagine

Imagine that you have been invited to a huge music concert. You are very excited to be going. It is a prestigious event and tickets sold out a long time ago. It is to be held in a huge arena, big enough to seat the thousands of people attending. When you arrive the noise is deafening – so many people! You eventually find your seat and sit down expectantly. Suddenly a man appears on stage at the microphone. He announces that there are envelopes under every seat and that there is a very special prize on offer. A lucky person is to be allowed backstage after the event to meet the famous musicians and to attend an after-show party as a guest of honour. The announcer says that the person who has the envelope containing a piece of paper with a star printed on it is the winner.

Everyone immediately looks for their envelope and rips it open. You open yours and can't believe your eyes. On it is a printed star! You jump out of your seat and begin to wave it excitedly. Then you notice that the person next to you and the next person along are waving their pieces of paper excitedly, too. In fact, everyone in the stadium is waving a piece of paper with a star printed on it. The announcer steps up to the microphone once again. 'That's right,' he shouts with a huge grin, 'everyone's invited to the party!'

How did you feel when you imagined this scene? Did you think you would or would not find a star on the piece of paper under your seat? How did you feel when you found it? How did you feel when you realized everyone else had a star, too?

Can you believe that, like a huge party to which everyone is invited, God's compassion includes everyone? What might your meditation tell you about your own thoughts on compassion?

Prayer

God of care and love, no one can measure the height, depth, length or breadth of your love, for it is like an immeasurable ocean. It cannot be exhausted or drained. I need your compassion, especially when I am weak. But I also want to show your compassion to others around me, who may need it today. Help me to draw on your great resources of compassion, to be refreshed myself and to allow that same refreshing to come to others. Amen.

Poem

Walk the life

Taste the terror of the persecuted.
Have what is yours unjustly stripped away.
Experience life as a violent threat.

Be utterly betrayed.

Know what it is to work
As one on whom others relentlessly rely.
Fear your home will be destroyed.

Learn all these things:

To become more human.
To love more honestly.
To grow more holy.

Inspirations

Our souls sit close and silently within,
And their own web from their own entrails spin;
And when eyes meet far off, our sense is such,
That, spider like, we feel the tenderest touch.

John Dryden

He watch'd and wept, he pray'd and felt for all.

Oliver Goldsmith

Yet, taught by time, my heart has learned to glow
For other's good, and melt at other's woe.

Homer

Never elated while one man's oppress'd;
Never dejected while another's blessed.

Alexander Pope

He who feels no compassion will become insane.

Proverb

Strengthen me by sympathizing with my strength not my weakness.

Amos Bronson Alcott

Pity and need
Make all flesh kin.
There is no caste in blood.

Edwin Arnold

A heart at leisure from itself,
To soothe and sympathize.

Anna Letitia Waring

A sympathetic heart is like a spring of pure water bursting forth from the mountain side.

Anonymous

Man may dismiss compassion from his heart, but God never will.

William Cowper

Open hands to receive

Several months ago I was asked to interview Stella, a woman who had set up a community project that worked with disadvantaged families. It was the usual brief: 1,500 words plus photos. Stella greeted me warmly in the small office where she worked. 'I started with just a mobile phone and had to get on with it,' she began, laughing. Today Stella runs a project that employs almost thirty people, and our work relationship has grown, too.

Since that initial interview, I have done media work for the project, as well as discussing publicity strategies, photographing countless children and families, and writing leaflets and posters advertizing the project. At every stage, all it took to see our work grow (discounting the blood, sweat and tears) was a simple 'yes' – a 'yes' to opportunity.

Our lives are like this, I think. Opportunities come our way and we are constantly challenged to discern whether 'yes' or 'no' is the right response. These days, I tend to err on the side of 'yes'. When it comes to opportunity, I like adventure. True, burn-out can come from saying 'yes' to too many things too much of the time. But disillusion and boredom can come when we say 'yes' to too few.

On another occasion, I had just finished writing a book called *Paths Through Grief*. It had been a demanding book to write and, in a sense, to relive. But on the very morning I finished it, I received a phone call from a magazine editor for whom I sometimes write. She asked me if I would be willing to interview a lady who managed a sports complex and had set up a team of women tennis players, who call themselves 'The Pink Ladies'.

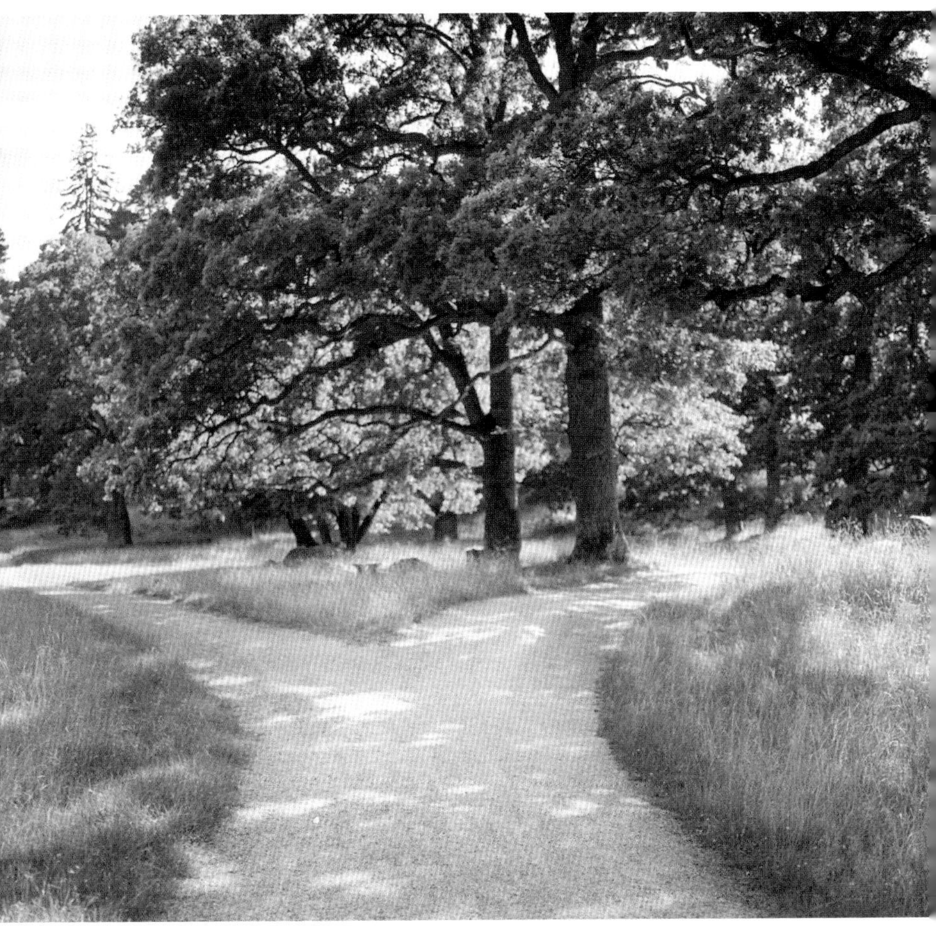

The proposal made me laugh, and was so different from the book I had just written that I said 'yes'.

I met Di at the sports centre where she was manager and we immediately hit it off. In the course of interviewing her, I told her how I used to play a lot of tennis – in fact, as a teenager I spent hours hitting a ball against a wall and regularly played tennis with a friend until it was too dark to play any more. I had forgotten how passionate I used to be about sport, but talking to Di reminded me. Di immediately offered me a free coaching session and promised to give me advice about a long-standing ankle injury, which I thought precluded me from playing sport seriously again. A few weeks later, a friend of a friend also offered to play tennis with me, and as well as having a great knock-around, we became friends, too.

I'm beginning to realize that life is less like a series of one-off events than a set of interlinked strands. One thing flows to another, which flows to another and then another. In this way, life gifts us with its own momentum. Sometimes all we're invited to do is get into the river of life and see where it will take us. Recognizing this and saying 'yes' to opportunity becomes a delight in itself. No longer do we fret about summoning up enough energy to start everything afresh every time. Instead, life issues us a new, bold challenge, which to my ears sounds something like this: 'Jump in!'

Delight and invitation are important elements of life. Of course, it is often the divine who is behind the best, most exciting opportunities we receive, and we are invited to say 'yes' and to delight in whatever those opportunities are – be they personal or public. But we may also have a sense of anticipation about what this will bring to us in the future. The seeds of our greatest endeavours may be in what we choose to say 'yes' to now. Life, the divine, is always giving to us. Sometimes, all we may have to do is open our hands in gratitude to receive.

Meditation

Read

I have come that they may have life, and have it abundantly.

John 10:10

But the Lord said to me, 'Do not say, "I am only a youth"; for to all to whom I send you you shall go, and whatever I command you, you shall speak.'

Jeremiah 1:7

The wisdom of a prudent man is to discern his way, but the folly of fools is deceiving.

Proverbs 14:8

Consider

Do you believe that the divine intends you to have abundant life? What might that life look like for you right now?

How might you like to develop a more open-minded approach to life? Do you put obstacles or excuses in the path of opportunities that come your way? Jeremiah initially cited his young age as a reason not to take the opportunities that the divine presented to him.

How might you develop the gift of discernment in your own life? What is your image of wisdom? Does it include the possibility of finding solutions and ways forward? Where would you like to exercise prudence today?

Imagine

Imagine that you have been given a huge fruit bowl. It is full of very varied-looking fruit. You choose one and hold it in your hands. Notice what it looks like – its colour, shape and texture. Now you eat some of the fruit. Is it easy to eat or hard, perhaps, to peel? What does the fruit taste and smell like? You notice, as you eat more of the fruit, that it contains pips. What do they look like? Will you save them and plant them out or throw them away?

What did your meditation tell you about your attitude to receptivity? Perhaps you chose the largest, most beautiful fruit. Did its taste live up to your expectations? Or maybe you chose a small, ugly fruit. Why do you think you did this? Did its taste outmatch its appearance? And what did you decide to do with the pips from the fruit you had eaten? Perhaps you decided to keep them and to plant them out. Or maybe you felt that planting them out would be too much effort or that you did not have the skills or the knowledge to make them grow.

Reflect on what your meditation tells you about your receptivity to situations you are currently facing, and about your confidence that you can bring something good out of them.

Prayer

God of wisdom, sometimes you want me to jump right into life, to get in the flow of it and be carried along. At other times you counsel a slower, more prudent approach. Help me to know, today, when to give my 'yes' and when to hold it back. Help me to see my way forward, guided always by your wisdom. Thank you for every opportunity that you bring my way, and that you often want to support or even carry me through my day. Energize me. Amen.

Poem

Ms Dynamite

I dare you.

Speak what you really want to speak.
Touch who you really want to touch.
Hold what you really want to hold.
Live how you really want to live.

Be as incendiary as you like.

Inspirations

Know thine opportunity.

Pittacus of Mitylene

A crisis is an opportunity riding the dangerous wind.

Chinese proverb

To find out what one is fitted to do, and to secure an opportunity to do it, is the key to happiness.

Bishop Richard Cumberland

He that will not when he may,
When he will he shall have nay.

Robert Burton

Opportunity is missed by most people because it is dressed in overalls and looks like work.

Abraham Cowley

Seek not for fresher founts afar,
Just drop your bucket where you are;
And while the ship right onward leaps,
Uplift it from the exhaustless deeps.
Parch not your life with dry despair;
The stream of hopes flow everywhere.
So under every sky and star,
Just drop your bucket where you are.

Anonymous

Let us seize, friends, our opportunity from the day as it passes.

Horace

A wise man will make more opportunities than he finds.

Francis Bacon

The pessimist sees difficulty in every opportunity. The optimist sees the opportunity in every difficulty.

Winston Churchill

Any human anywhere will blossom in a hundred unexpected talents and capacities simply by being given the opportunity to do so.

Doris Lessing

Seize opportunity by the beard, for it is bald behind.

Proverb

Anyone can count the seeds in an apple.
Only God can count the apples in a seed.

Robert Schuller

There is a history in all men's lives,
Figuring the nature of the times deceased,
The which observed, a man may prophesy,
With a near aim, of the main chance of things
As yet not come to life, which in their seeds
And weak beginnings lie intreasured.

William Shakespeare

It is difficult to say what is impossible,
for the dream of yesterday is the hope of today
and the reality of tomorrow.

Robert H. Goddard

On reflection

Not long ago I received an email from a particularly difficult contact. It was demanding, pressuring and not a little manipulative. On the other hand, I had compassion for this person who was emailing me. There were tricky problems to consider. I wasn't sure what I could say that would be helpful. My mind was agitating with all sorts of ideas, so I decided to take some time out. I sat and

reflected for a while. I listened to my heart: what was I really thinking and feeling? What would be the wise thing to do in this situation? I heard my heart say, 'Be cautious'. And I knew, instinctively, that this was the life-giving solution for me.

Then I recalled a recent conversation with a family member. We had remembered how I thought about buying a particular house, but had had a strong gut reaction against it. There was no obvious reason for my gut reaction: the house was sound; the owners were keen to sell and to sell to me; the street was nice, and near to the amenities I wanted. So why did I feel so strongly against it? It wasn't until months later that the reason became clear -- a reason I could not have envisaged at the time I was considering the purchase. But to buy that house at that time would probably have spelt disaster for me. Sometimes it pays to honour the wisdom of our hearts or at least to take it into account.

Receptivity may help us to say 'yes' to life-giving opportunities, but that doesn't mean we should say 'yes' to everything. To learn the potency of our 'yes' – and also our 'no' – we may want to develop the art of wise reflection. We cannot condone, for example, injustice, violence, greed or evil. So how do we discern what to say 'yes' and what to say 'no' to? By our choices, we are building a good life or a not so good life.

For active people, reflection is important. I have a beautiful card in my workspace which reminds me of this. It's a photograph of a piece of land art: a bridge of pebbles arching over clear water, whose reflection makes a perfect circle. For me it represents how the balance of activity and reflection can create something beautiful and whole.

Part of this balance and discernment comes as we learn to listen. We may want to develop a kind of deep listening – listening with the heart. Recently I have discovered my own heart to be a source of wisdom and insight. When problems or challenges perplex me, I have realized the need to still myself and to reflect. As I reflect more deeply, I find that wisdom arises gently from my own heart – a discernment that can guide and shape my outward actions. It's just this insight which helps us to live with greater integrity and purpose.

This kind of listening doesn't need to involve an extended time of quiet – although it may do. Sometimes it's simply a case of not having a knee-jerk reaction. Sometimes all it takes is five or ten minutes of stillness that will allow us to get in touch with the rivers of grace and wisdom within us. In a culture that demands immediacy and definiteness, it may be a strange discipline at first. But the very action of not allowing ourselves to become pressured and knocked off-centre may be beneficial in itself.

I don't always get the balance right. Sometimes life is a whirr of activity and deadlines. I lose focus. At other times, I waste too much time dreaming and daydreaming, when a bit of hard work might be more beneficial. But gradually, I think I'm discerning a rhythm to my life. When I get the mix of activity and reflection right, everything seems to flow with greater ease and joy and my actions seem to be more authentic, more grounded and, often, more loving.

Meditation

Read

When Daniel knew that the document had been signed, he went to his house where he had windows in his upper chamber open toward Jerusalem; and he got down upon his knees three times a day and prayed and gave thanks before his God, as he had done previously.

Daniel 6:10

To make an apt answer is a joy to a man, and a word in season, how good it is!

Proverbs 15:23

For everything there is a season, and a time for every matter under heaven: a time to be born, and a time to die; a time to plant, and a time to pluck up what is planted; a time to kill, and a time to heal; a time to break down, and a time to build up; a time to weep, and a time to laugh; a time to mourn, and a time to dance; a time to cast away stones, and a time to gather stones together; a time to embrace, and a time to refrain from embracing; a time to seek, and a time to lose; a time to keep, and a time to cast away; a time to rend, and a time to sew; a time to keep silence, and a time to speak; a time to love, and a time to hate; a time for war, and a time for peace.

Ecclesiastes 3:1-8

Consider

Daniel chose to have a rhythm of life that included praying three times a day. He chose this even at times of great stress. What kind of rhythm would you like to have in your day? Could you write out a rhythm of life that includes space for reflection, meditation, contemplation or even taking a nap?

Have you ever experienced the joy of giving an

appropriate piece of advice at just the right time? Can you identify what it was that made you successful?

The writer of Ecclesiastes declares that there is a season for everything. Can you name the season you are passing through right now?

Imagine

Imagine a pear tree, full of fruit. You notice one particular pear, which is ripening in the rain and the sun. When it is ready, a hand reaches out and carefully picks it, gently placing it with other ripe pears in a basket. In the basket, the pear is safely stored and kept until it is needed. On another day, a hand reaches into the basket and pulls out your pear. It is ripe and juicy, full of fresh goodness and ready to eat.

Can you imagine that pear is like an idea, growing and ripening within you? An idea may lie within you for some time, out of immediate sight. A time of reflection may give you and your idea the darkness, storage and safety they need to grow. Then when the time comes, you can reach into the storeroom of your mind or heart and pull out a fully-ripened idea. Can you believe that reflection is the process which allows all of these stages to happen?

Prayer

God of wholeness, you love it when my life has a rhythm and a balance which blesses me and blesses others. Help me to get in sync with your rhythm in my life. Help me to know when to do and when not to do, when to work and when to rest, when to speak and when to stay silent. Season-giver, in you everything turns at its right time. Bless me whether I rise or lie down. Amen.

Poem

Walk in the woods

You lay me down
In fields of flaxen grass,
Amid roaming deer,
Where the grasshopper sings.

You lay me down
In woods of soft green,
Amid the calling crows,
Where slow clouds sail the sky.

You lay me down,

So all the heat of my days
Seeps into the cool earth
And I think and feel
And breathe again.

Inspirations

Knowledge of the self is the mother of all knowledge. So it is incumbent on me to know my self, to know it completely, to know its minutiae, its characteristics, its subtleties, and its very atoms.

Kahlil Gibran

The learn'd reflect on what before they knew.

Alexander Pope

For take thy ballaunce if thou be so wise,
And weigh the winds that under heaven doth blow;
Or weigh the light that in the east doth rise;
Or weigh the thought that from man's mind doth flow.

Edmund Spenser

A soul without reflection, like a pile
Without inhabitant, to ruin runs.

Edward Young

By three methods we may learn wisdom: first, by reflection, which is the noblest; second, by imitation, which is the easiest; and third, by experience, which is the bitterest.

Confucius

The workings of the human heart are the profoundest mystery of the universe. One moment they make us despair of our kind, and the next we see in them the reflection of the divine image.

Charles W. Chesnutt

Happiness is not a matter of intensity but of balance and order and rhythm and harmony.

Thomas Merton

People with great gifts are easy to find, but symmetrical and balanced ones never.

Ralph Waldo Emerson

Man always travels along precipices. His truest obligation is to keep his balance.

Pope John Paul II

Something in human nature causes us to start slacking off at our moment of greatest accomplishment. As you become successful, you will need a great deal of self-discipline not to lose your sense of balance, humility and commitment.

H. Ross Perot

When you cannot make up your mind which of two evenly balanced courses of action you should take – choose the bolder.

W. J. Slim

The rhythm of life is intricate but orderly, tenacious but fragile. To keep that in mind is to build the key to survival.

Shirley Hufstedler

A moment's insight is sometimes worth a life's experience.

Thomas Fuller

An ocean of wonder

I have a large photograph hanging in my bedroom. It shows a rather drab, grey lighthouse in the middle of a shifting emerald ocean. Three or four great atlantic rollers bear energetically down on the lighthouse. But I didn't buy the picture for the lighthouse. I bought it because of the way the light transfuses the waves. Through the first of these huge waves, sunlight filters like light through the veined, green leaves of a large plant. It's truly beautiful.

But the photograph inspires me in other ways, too. There's a regularity and a reliability about the way the waves appear. I've heard that surfers say waves come in threes and the last wave is always the biggest. I like the idea of this kind of predictability. While the waves are sublimely beautiful and awe-inspiring, each different from the last, I like the idea that if a wave passes, another will come.

I guess I look at those waves in a symbolic sense. The waves remind me that the divine is always supremely generous: that wave after wave of opportunity comes and, like a surfer, I can choose which waves I want to surf today. Such invitations excite me and make me sense that at the heart of the divine exists a huge sense of wonderful play.

Of course, if you want to surf you need concentration, balance, commitment and not a little bit of nerve. Just the attributes you need to live a day well! But also on offer is an exhilarating ride. Fear and stress turn to wonder and joy. True, we won't always get it right. We'll fall off the waves of opportunity we try to ride. We may even be mashed by the waves. Life can be bruising as

well as exhilarating. Yet, truth be told, I'd rather be under the waves than sitting on the beach.

When I lived in Israel for a time, a popular weekend activity involved riding the River Jordan in great rubber rings. The knack of a successful ride, I was told, was not to let your feet drag too deeply in the water but to allow yourself to go, literally, with the flow.

Cultivating a sense of wonder requires exactly the same attitude. It's about not digging our feet in when the current of life wants to rush us on, to exhilarate us. It's about giving up our rigid stubbornness, our fear, our desire constantly to control the outcome. It's about getting into the river or the sea of life, with all its currents and all its power and all its flow, and allowing ourselves to be borne along. This makes for true awe and wonder.

Meditation

Read

He said to the paralytic, 'I say to you, rise, take up your pallet and go home.' And he rose, and immediately took up the pallet and went out before them all; so that they were all amazed and glorified God, saying, 'We never saw anything like this!'

Mark 2:10–12

The whole world stands in awe of the great things that you have done. Your deeds bring shouts of joy from one end of the earth to the other.

Psalm 65:8

When I look at your heavens, the work of your fingers, the moon and the stars that you have established, what are human beings that you are mindful of them, mortals that you care for them? Yet you have made them a little lower than God, and crowned them with glory and honour.

Psalm 8:3–5

Consider

When did you last experience wonder? Has your sense of wonder ever led to a sense of the divine? Would you like it to?

What effect do wonder and awe have on you? How does it feel to experience them, or how have you expressed them? They can be powerful emotions.

What causes wonder to rise up in you? Perhaps, like the Psalmist, it is when you consider creation. If you know that certain situations cause you great wonder (for example, an amazing landscape or the giftedness of a friend), you might like deliberately to seek them out for the expanded sense of life and the divine they can bring to you.

Imagine

Imagine that you are a canoeist about to start a white-water race. Before you is a mass of swirling, energetic white-water. The signal to start is given. You propel yourself forwards into the powerful water. It wants to drive you this way and that. You must concentrate hard, using your paddle to steer the canoe and occasionally to push yourself through the water. You must also use your whole body to balance the canoe and keep it from capsizing. Finally, after negotiating several hazards, you make it over the finish line.

How did you feel at the beginning of this meditation before the race started? Maybe you felt nervous, excited, worried or bold? Name your feelings. When you contemplated the water, what did you think? As you started the race, all your concentration may have been given to staying upright and not capsizing. Are there situations in your life right now that demand this kind of undivided attention? What might be the benefits of giving this attention?

How successful were you in your canoe ride – did you capsize, fall into the water, crash into rocks? Athletes talk of developing a positive mental attitude to win. Did you have this or do you see a need to develop it? How did you feel when you passed the finish line? Perhaps some of these feelings are highlighting the way you feel about challenging situations in your life right now. Can you bring those situations and your feelings about them to the divine honestly and openly?

Prayer

God of wonder, you are the tree of life. Everything is fruitful in you. Let me fall into a state of wonder. Let me fall into you and your beautiful, majestic, wonderful creation. Life is a wonderful, challenging, demanding, exhausting, fulfilling ride. You see all the situations in my life and long to bless me through all of them, even the most difficult ones. Help me to be open to you and the wonders you can do. Amen.

Poem

Love your life

Wander

Under January blue skies,
With staunch and fierce friends
And warm food in your belly.

Wander
Beneath black mountains,
Where silence grows
And your mind touches soft rest.

Be a witness

To beauty, glory, truth
Wherever you happen to find it.

Wonder
Wherever you happen to find it.

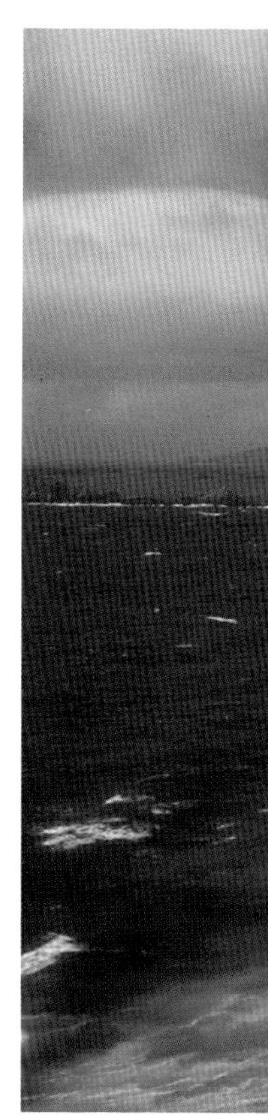

Inspirations

Men go abroad to wonder at the heights of mountains, at the huge waves of the sea, at the long courses of the rivers, at the vast compass of the ocean, at the circular motions of the stars, and they pass by themselves without wondering.

St Augustine

Philosophy begins in wonder. And, at the end, when philosophic thought has done its best, the wonder remains.

Alfred North Whitehead

The larger the island of knowledge, the longer the shoreline of wonder.

Ralph W. Sockman

A child's world is fresh and new and beautiful, full of wonder and excitement. It is our misfortune that for most of us that clear-eyed vision, that true instinct for what is beautiful and awe-inspiring, is dimmed and even lost before we reach adulthood.

Rachel Carson

Men love to wonder and that is the seed of science.

Ralph Waldo Emerson

He who can no longer pause to wonder and stand rapt in awe is as good as dead. His eyes are closed.

Albert Einstein

Wonder is the basis of worship.

Thomas Carlyle

He who wonders discovers that this in itself is wonder.

M. C. Escher

I am touched but not broken by the waves.

Proverb

Stuff your eyes with wonder... live as if you'd drop dead in ten seconds. See the world. It's more fantastic than any dream made or paid for in factories.

Ray Bradbury

It was through the feeling of wonder that men now and at first began to philosophize.

Aristotle

God moves in a mysterious way,
His wonders to perform;
He plants his footsteps in the sea,
And rides upon the storm.

William Cowper

The world will never starve for want of wonders, but for want of wonder.

G. K. Chesterton

Wisdom begins in wonder.

Socrates

Feel the beauty

Recently, a friend came to visit for the weekend. We stayed up into the early hours, talking, eating, laughing and star-gazing. Next day we loaded a bag with picnic food, the Saturday papers and a rug, then headed for the local country park. It was a beautiful, hot, sunny day. We walked (not very far) and flopped onto the rug in the dappled delight of a nearby clearing.

Lying in the blissful sunshine, I turned to my friend and said, 'You know, I love the sunshine. Somehow it gets into your body and makes you feel full of light.' She turned to me with a grin and said, 'Of course it does. Doesn't it make something good inside your body?' She was right. Sunshine creates vitamin D in our bodies, which is essential for healthy bones and, scientists suggest, a player in preventing some cancers.

Every beauty, including sunshine, is good for us in a profound way – good for our souls, our minds, our hearts and our bodies. We revel in the delight of a beautiful landscape. Yet I don't live in what is traditionally regarded as a picturesque part of the UK. The Midlands aren't renowned for their dramatic seascapes, for quiet and cosy villages or even for gently rolling pastureland, although I've been lucky enough to experience all of these landscapes and more. Tourists don't flock to my neck of the woods and local shops don't stock a plethora of postcards celebrating my area's obvious beauty.

Yet I can't deny that I haven't, at times, been enchanted by the way certain trees stride down a field of yellow corn or the way a bank of clouds rolls like the perfect artistic backdrop to a shimmering landscape. Such

snapshots of beauty are nothing special, yet at the same time *everything* about them is special. And I practise photography, not merely for the art of it, but because it causes me to pay attention to beauty, to contemplate it fully, to enter into it more profoundly.

If we can find a way to contemplate and connect with beauty – maybe by playing within it or observing it from a place of stillness and receptivity – we may find our hearts soaring, our spirits lifting, our experience of reverence deepening. We may even find messages of divine goodness encoded in such beauty, just waiting for our contemplation to decipher them.

While on a walk with my small son recently, he excitedly invited me to climb a steep, ferny bank to inspect in more detail a gnarled tree which was rooted there. The adult me looked at the bank with weariness, more concerned with whether we would finish our walk in good time. But I agreed, to avoid disappointing my son. Clambering among the roots of the tree, we spotted several small snails clinging to its bark. Their shells were beautiful whorls of colour: chocolate, caramel, strawberry mousse. Somehow they spoke a silent message to me about the beauty of slowness – and this at a time when my life was particularly pressured and busy.

We can contemplate beauty for the sheer joy of it, for a delighted awareness of what simply is. But we can penetrate beauty too, as a bee penetrates a flower, to find succour and sweet food for our spirits.

In this way any part of creation, however majestic or humble, can become a bearer of sweet wisdom to us. Beauty enfolds wisdom lightly within it and it does not take much effort from us to extract that wisdom. As I write, I'm at the tail-end of a particularly hectic season. It's high summer and the three horse chestnuts I can see over the rooftops from my kitchen window are in their full-leaved glory. They remind me that, after a season of growth, it's all right to rest. Even in rest, the trees are home to small insects, shelter to animals and humans, and food for birds.

And we ourselves are beautifully and wisely made. Not by the narrow definitions of cosmetic beauty that our culture likes to pump out at us, but by the definition of our souls and spirits. Each one of us carries a divine mark in us and that divine mark, by its very essence, is always beautiful. I want to safeguard and celebrate that beauty, too, opposing injustice, oppression and the exploitation of others.

A few days ago I opened my door to the elderly gentleman who had sold me his house. We had arranged for him to come for a cup of tea and advise me about the tangle of raspberries, strawberries and plum trees which had been, literally, his fruitful legacy to me. I opened the door and in his characteristic, laid-back, Caribbean drawl, he greeted me with a blessing: 'Hello, beautiful girl!' he grinned.

To call forth the inherent beauty in another is an act of love of which we are all capable. I wonder how it might colour our relationships, even the most challenging ones, to know that we are all capable of great beauty today?

Meditation

Read

The heavens tell of the glory of God. The skies display his marvelous craftsmanship. Day after day they continue to speak; night after night they make him known. They speak without a sound or a word; their voice is silent in the skies; yet their message has gone out to all the earth, and their words to all the world. The sun lives in the heavens where God placed it. It bursts forth like a radiant bridegroom after his wedding. It rejoices like a great athlete eager to run the race. The sun rises at one end of the heavens and follows its course to the other end. Nothing can hide from its heat.

Psalm 19:1–6

Out of Zion, the perfection of beauty, God shines forth.

Psalm 50:2

Ah, you are beautiful, my love; ah, you are beautiful; your eyes are doves. Ah, you are beautiful, my beloved, truly lovely. Our couch is green...

Song of Songs 1:15–16

Consider

Take a walk. Even in the depths of a city, trees blossom, birds sing, flowers grace the face of the earth. What messages are they sending to you today?

Have you experienced the divine as beautiful? Can you believe your soul, likewise, carries the undeniable and beautiful fingerprints of the divine creator?

Can you view the divine as being, at heart, a lover? Can you believe that your soul can be the object of the divine's ardent admiration?

Imagine

Imagine the most beautiful thing you can. Perhaps it is an inanimate object – a painting, vase or antique? Or maybe it is an animal or insect – a leopard, a butterfly or a swan? Or perhaps it is a particular landscape or skyscape? Look closely at what you are contemplating. Consider its shape, colours, form and movement. See it in all its fullness and all its detail. Let your eye rove at leisure around what you are contemplating. Allow any feelings – perhaps of admiration or delight – to rise to the surface too.

Now imagine that this thing of beauty is you. You share characteristics of beauty with whatever it was that you were contemplating. Think about the feelings that arose when you imagined this object of beauty. Can you believe that the divine feels the same when it thinks about you? You are beautifully and wonderfully created by the same divine hand.

If you want to take the meditation further, you might like to consider whether there were particular things that you admired in your contemplation which the divine may want to draw to your attention. For example, if you imagined a scene of great peace, could this be telling you that you particularly love peace and are capable of great peace yourself? Or if you thought of a tiger, that you are capable of great speed and agility, be it physical or mental? What might your meditation be communicating to you in a deeper way?

Prayer

God of beauty, I see your fingerprints in everything around me. Open my eyes more and more to this beauty. I do not want to escape from your world, but to penetrate it even more deeply, to find your messages of love and care within it. Give me wisdom to decipher what you are saying. Help me to be both a bearer and a caller-forth of beauty today. Amen.

Poem

Transformation

We walked on water to the piazza,
Our toes shimmering and bright.
For a moment pigeons became doves
In the incandescent light.

Inspirations

I've never seen a smiling face that was not beautiful.

Anonymous

That which is striking and beautiful is not always good, but that which is good is always beautiful.

Ninon de L'Enclos

Some people, no matter how old they get, never lose their beauty – they merely move it from their faces into their hearts.

Martin Buxbaum

What humbugs we are, who pretend to live for Beauty, but never see the Dawn!

Logan Pearsall Smith

The most beautiful view is the one I share with you.

Anonymous

When you have only two pennies left in the world, buy a loaf of bread with one and a lily with the other.

Chinese proverb

The soul that sees beauty may sometimes walk alone.

Goethe

You don't love a woman because she is beautiful. She is beautiful because you love her.

Anonymous

Remember that the most beautiful things in the world are the most useless: peacocks and lilies for instance.

John Ruskin

Beauty is a shadow of God on the universe.

Gabriela Mistral

The joy ethic

I was always being told off at school for messing about with my friends. Unfortunately it's a joy ethic that's never entirely been squashed out of me – despite innumerable and frowning attempts to do so. I can't help it and, in truth, I don't want to help it. I love joy. I love laughter. I love the sense of strength and health they bring and the connection and community they can engender.

And so I seem to take this joy ethic into everything I do. People say, 'Don't mix business with pleasure', but my secret work vision is only to work with friends – turning colleagues into friends and friends into colleagues. Why should we believe that work should always be a po-faced affair?

Working as a staffer once at a charity, I stumbled across a book about disaster management – how to cope, for example, in situations of great conflict, instability or threat, such as refugee camps or in countries suffering violent unrest. On a quiet afternoon, I flicked through this handbook, written by a veteran in the field of disaster management. One whole chapter, to my great surprise, was devoted to the importance of humour, laughter and joy. Imagine that: amid the horrors of genocide, violence, threat and desperate conflict, people of great skills, compassion and talent are being encouraged to experience joy.

People may argue that there is a time for joy, but not when people are suffering. I agree that compassionate tears are a powerful witness, but I'm not convinced that joy has no place in hardship. Personally, during the most challenging times in my life I've needed and appreciated friends who 'tell it like it is', as funny, straight and poignant as that may be. To laugh through tears is like glimpsing a rainbow on the edge of dark clouds: somehow our hearts are lifted.

Moreover, when going through difficult times in my own life, I have been deeply challenged about my own attitudes to joy. I've seen that I can allow my circumstances to dictate my mood to me – to be down when circumstances are bad and up when they are good. Yet to do so only makes me a prisoner of fate, a victim of circumstance. Following this course merely puts us on a permanent rollercoaster – forever going up and down.

Instead, I have been challenged to see that it is possible to choose joy deliberately, and to do so may be profoundly liberating. Circumstances are always shifting, always changing, even within a single day. To live in an unhealthily sensitive way to such changes may make us unstable, unhappy and anxious. Yet to live with an attitude of joy and hope helps us to transcend these shifting sands.

So how can we begin to live in this way? I think maybe it all starts with hearing from within us the divine invitation to deep joy. We discover in our hearts both our great desire and capacity for joy. 'Fill me with your joy,'

we can say boldly to the divine – and we may find that it becomes just so.

This does not mean that we will become insensitive to the needs or difficulties of others – far from it. Joy is not a shield that protects us from hardship or difficulty. Rather, it's like a refreshing stream within us, which helps us to cope with and overcome the inevitable stresses of each day. In doing so, we enter into the happiness that is shared at the heart of the divine. We discover that laughter heals and that joy strengthens. We experience and become the bearers of a freeing and healing joy. Messing about may, on occasion, be just what our suffering world needs.

Meditation

Read

When the Lord restored the fortunes of Zion, we were like
those who dream.
Then our mouth was filled with laughter, and our tongue
with shouts of joy;
then it was said among the nations, 'The Lord has done
great things for them.'
The Lord has done great things for us, and we rejoiced.

Psalm 126:1–3

Then he said to them, 'Go your way, eat the fat and drink sweet wine and send portions of them to those for whom nothing is prepared, for this day is holy to our Lord; and do not be grieved, for the joy of the Lord is your strength.'

Nehemiah 8:10

You show me the path of life.
In your presence there is fullness of joy;
in your right hand are pleasures for evermore.

Psalm 16:11

Consider

Can you believe God wants to fill your mouth with laughter (notice there are no half-measures)? How might it change you to believe that God, although deeply compassionate, is also a God of great joy and laughter?

Can you recall times when you felt strengthened by joy and laughter? What were you doing, where were you, who were you with? Can you create such occasions on a regular basis and be open-handed and open-hearted about who is with you?

Have you ever had a spiritual experience where you tasted great joy? Would you like to? Can you believe God delights in the celebrations of your heart and does not frown on them?

Imagine

Imagine that you are being led by a host into a room where there is a long table. On the table, covered at present with a cloth, are all sorts of intriguing bumps and bulges, but you have no idea what they are yet. What's more, you notice as you enter the room that sitting in front of the table is a group of unsmiling, serious-looking people. Some of them are frowning and looking at you in a disapproving manner.

Your host motions for you to sit at the table, facing this joyless crowd of people. You sit in a chair and as you do so, your host pulls off the tablecloth. You can't believe what you are seeing! The table is groaning under the weight of all your favourite food and drink. There are a few stray presents dotted around the table, with tags bearing your name. Your host motions for you to take what you like. But still you sit facing the crowd, whose disapproval only seems to have deepened at the sight of your feast. What will you do?

Go slowly through your meditation again. How did you feel as you entered the room? Did you recognize particular faces in the crowd of ill-wishers? How did you feel when you were invited to sit facing them before, and after, the unveiling of the feast? Did you obey your host and indulge in the feast or did anything hold you back from doing so?

What might your meditation be telling you about your capacity to enjoy and celebrate, especially at the invitation of the divine? If you felt inhibited by particular people, do you know why?

Prayer

God of wisdom, how great you are that you make even laughter good for us! Thank you that we are not merely victims of the circumstances of our lives, but can rise above them. Thank you that your joy heals, creates and sustains. Fill me with joy and fill my mouth with laughter. Protect and create a right sense of fun in my life. Amen.

Poem

Smiling in the rain

Walking that damp morning
Down the drizzly street,
I remember
Joy, like a dance in my bones.

I turned to you,
I remember,
I said:

'For a long time
I thought my whole being
Was about peace,
But this joy, this laughter...'

And so I began,
Now loose-limbed,
To stand tall and dance.

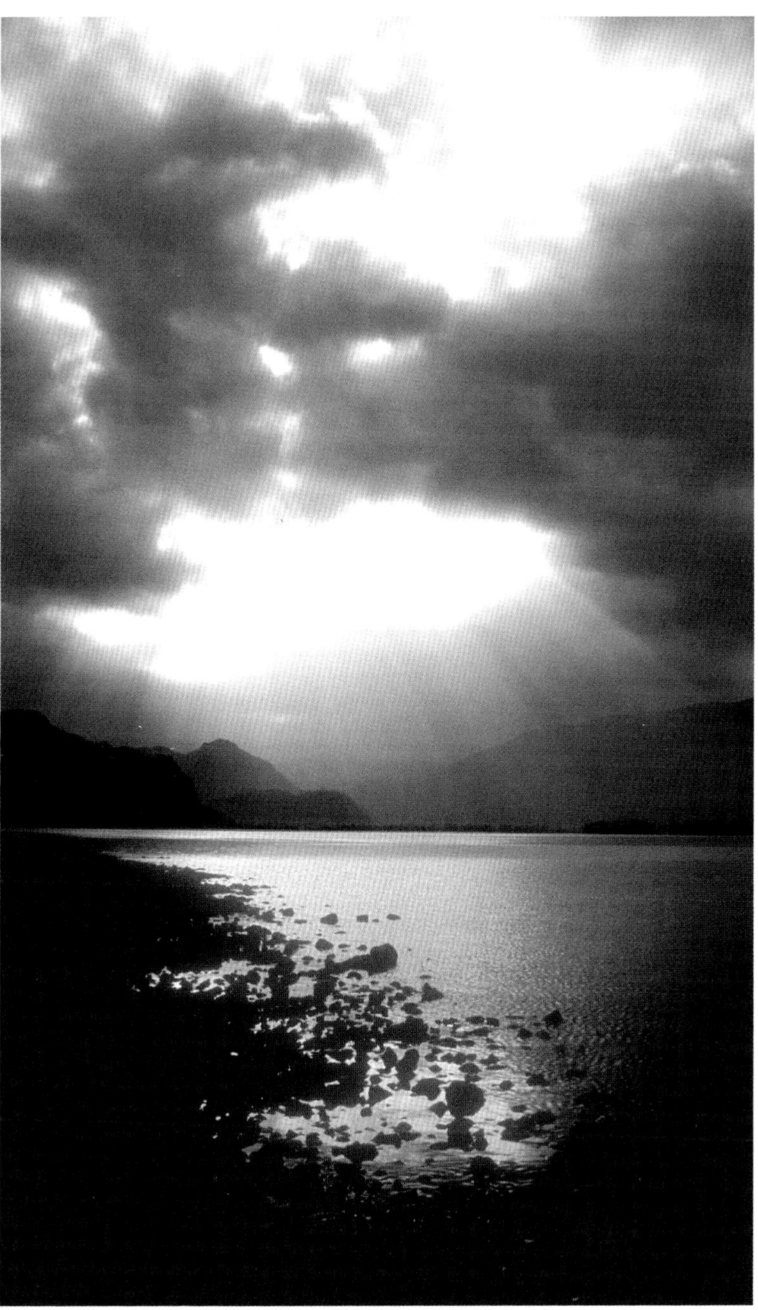

Inspirations

Man is fond of counting his troubles, but he does not count his joys. If he counted them up as he ought to, he would see that every lot has enough happiness provided for it.

Fyodor Dostoyevsky

Joy is a flower that blooms when you do.

Anonymous

One joy scatters a hundred griefs.

Chinese proverb

One filled with joy preaches without preaching.

Mother Teresa

If the day and night be such that you greet them with joy, and life emits a fragrance like flowers and sweet-scented herbs, more elastic, more starry, more immortal – that is your success. All nature is your congratulation and you have cause momentarily to bless yourself.

Henry David Thoreau

It is a comely fashion to be glad. Joy is the grace we say to God.

Jean Ingelow

All of us have had the experience of a sudden joy that came when nothing in the world had forewarned us of its coming – a joy so thrilling that if it was born of misery we remembered even the misery with tenderness.

Antoine de Saint-Exupéry

Who will tell whether one happy moment of love or the joy of breathing or walking on a bright morning and smelling the fresh air, is not worth all the suffering and effort which life implies?

Erich Fromm

There are souls in this world which have the gift of finding joy everywhere and of leaving it behind them when they go.

Frederick Faber

The aim of life is to live and to live means to be aware, joyously, drunkenly, serenely, divinely aware.

Henry Miller

Joy in one's heart and some laughter on one's lips is a sign that the person deep down has a pretty good grasp of life.

Hugh Sidey

Never trust people who tell you all their troubles but keep from you all their joys.

Proverb

Hold him alone truly fortunate who has ended his life in happy well-being.

Aeschylus

'Twas a jolly old pedagogue, long ago,
Tall and slender, and sallow and dry;
His form was bent, and his gait was slow,
His long thin hair was white as snow,
But a wonderful twinkle shone in his eye.
And he sang every night as he went to bed,
'Let us be happy down here below:
The living should live, though the dead be dead.'
Said the jolly old pedagogue long ago.

George Arnold

Happiness is good health and a bad memory.

Cesare di Bonesana Beccaria

Thus happiness depends, as Nature shows,
Less on exterior things than most suppose.

William Cowper

A mysterious doorway

I recently took on a new project which involved working with some of the most disadvantaged people in a community. I was desperately trying to find a photographer for the project when a friend gave me the number of a colleague of hers, Paul. He had recently changed careers to become a professional photographer. So I rang Paul's number, hopeful this could be the person the project needed and the project the person needed, glad to be the bearer of good news.

I spoke at length, enthusing about how interesting, varied and ultimately beneficial this work could be. Paul listened attentively, discussed the location and the fees amiably enough – and then turned the offer down. I was surprised. My friend had hinted that this type of work would be right up Paul's street and, as someone starting out on a creative career path, just the kind of offer he'd jump at. No doubt Paul had very good reasons for turning the opportunity down, but when I reflected on what had happened, I was challenged. How many opportunities do *I* turn down?

I remembered an invitation I had to work with another project. I didn't want to go; I wasn't inspired by the work; I very nearly turned the invitation down. But I went, and completely out of the blue, I was offered the kind of new challenge I'd secretly wanted for a while.

I'm not saying I get it right the whole time – far from it! And there's definitely a place for cautious discernment and healthy wisdom in our choice of pathways through life. But sometimes it may be right to cultivate a more open-handed, open-minded approach to life. It doesn't always come naturally. Truth be told, I'm the kind of person who always likes to sit in a forward-facing seat on a train – I like to know where I'm going and to make sure I'm getting there. Friends tease me that I read books backwards and it's true, I confess, I read the last page first – just to check it's a happy ending.

But life doesn't always work so neatly. Sometimes having everything worked out in the finest detail closes our options down rather than opening them up. Seeking permanent resolution, we narrow our lives down and, maybe, close ourselves to the grace of mystery.

A mystery is, by its very nature, not something that works out in a neat and tidy manner. I have discovered that life contains many such mysteries: suffering redeems us, strangers bless us, faith grows in trial, the persecuted rejoice and the humiliated of the world are its secret inheritors and heroes. Yet mystery rarely shouts about itself.

Instead, I think mystery is like a small, hidden doorway. It reminds me of a famous novel, *The Secret Garden*, whose main character languishes in ill health until he is led to a tiny, almost overgrown doorway in a wall, through which he stoops to enter into a garden of freedom and joy.

To enter the secret garden one must stoop. And in this I see a connection, too, between mystery and humility. Mystery, in just the same way, asks us to stoop, to let go of our clear-cut plans and precise definitions, which are sometimes little more than a form of pride or, perhaps, anxiety.

Instead it invites us to enter through the unprepossessing, even hidden, way. But maybe if we can accept the mysterious invitation today, we'll enter our own secret gardens, full of delights we could never have imagined. In this way, mystery becomes the hidden doorway through which we enter into a kind of blessed enchantment.

Meditation

Read

Even though our outer nature is wasting away, our inner nature is being renewed day by day. For this slight momentary affliction is preparing us for an eternal weight of glory beyond all measure, because we look not at what can be seen but at what cannot be seen; for what can be seen is temporary, but what cannot be seen is eternal.

2 Corinthians 4:16–18

Daniel said: 'Blessed be the name of God from age to age, for wisdom and power are his. He changes times and seasons, deposes kings and sets up kings; he gives wisdom to the wise and knowledge to those who have understanding. He reveals deep and hidden things; he knows what is in the darkness, and light dwells with him.'

Daniel 2:20–22

Listen, I will tell you a mystery! We will not all die, but we will all be changed, in a moment, in the twinkling of an eye, at the last trumpet. For the trumpet will sound, and the dead will be raised imperishable, and we will be changed.

For this perishable body must put on imperishability, and this mortal body must put on immortality.

1 Corinthians 15:51–53

Consider

How can you begin to look at what cannot be seen? What eternal mysteries might you be being invited to consider?

Can you believe that the divine is both the source of and the revealer of mysteries? What might it mean to you to know that the divine has mysteries to uncover to you?

If you could understand one mystery about the universe or human life, what would that one mystery be?

Imagine

Imagine that you are a famous scientist – perhaps Einstein or Edison. You have been working away for years at a particular problem. All your energies, all your concentration, all your education, even all of your funding, have been aimed at solving this one problem. You've encountered challenges, stresses, frustration, even ill health because of your quest. You've lost friends, status, money and maybe even your home because of your fixation on this one puzzle.

Then suddenly one day you have it! You've solved it! The enigma that has been puzzling you for so many years has unravelled itself and revealed its answer to you! You can hardly believe it. You check your calculations, but no, you are right! You have finally solved the mystery!

Now consider: what was the mystery you were trying to solve? Could you enter into the emotional struggle of trying to solve it? How did you feel on the day you hit upon the solution? Can you describe your feelings? How did the solution come to you and what might this be telling you about your natural inclination towards mystery (for example, you reached the solution after painstaking calculations, you dreamt the solution, friends helped you to solve it)? How do you feel knowing you have solved one of the greatest mysteries to baffle human minds (at least, in your meditation)? What mystery would you truly like to solve today? Would you dare to ask for divine assistance to do so?

Prayer

God of mystery, you invite me to enter a hidden way. You are a lover of good secrets and you like to surprise me. Help me to be humble. Help me to let go of my proud or anxious plans in order to embrace something greater. Take away the fears that prevent me from trusting you. Your every thought towards me is for good. Let me not miss a single blessing or beautiful surprise that you have planned for me. Amen.

Poem

Be free

Take off your own ideas,
Your times, constraints, views,

As one who deliberately undresses for bed.

Let other things be brought to you:
Work and people and places and friends,
Things that fit
This expanding life of yours.

Let yourself be clothed in new patterns,
New shapes.

They will delight you.
Allow it to be.

Inspirations

It is Lucifer,
The son of mystery;
And since God suffers him to be,
He, too, is God's minister,
And labors for some good
By us not understood.

Henry Wadsworth Longfellow

The important thing is not to stop questioning. Curiosity has its own reason for existing. One cannot help but be in awe when he contemplates the mysteries of eternity, of life, of the marvelous structure of reality. It is enough if one tries merely to comprehend a little of this mystery every day. Never lose a holy curiosity.

Albert Einstein

The universe is full of magical things patiently waiting for our wits to grow sharper.

Eden Phillpotts

When I was young, I said to God, 'God, tell me the mystery of the universe.' But God answered, 'That knowledge is for me alone.' So I said, 'God, tell me the mystery of the peanut.' Then God said, 'Well, George, that's more nearly your size.'

George Washington Carver

We are all, in a sense, experts on secrecy. From earliest childhood we feel its mystery and attraction. We know both the power it confers and the burden it imposes. We learn how it can delight, give breathing space and protect.

Sissela Bok

If a child is to keep alive his inborn sense of wonder, he needs the companionship of at least one adult who can share it, rediscovering with him the joy, excitement and mystery of the world we live in.

Rachel Carson

The only words that ever satisfied me as describing Nature are the terms used in fairy books, charm, spell, enchantment. They express the arbitrariness of the fact and its mystery.

G. K. Chesterton

Life consists in penetrating the unknown, and fashioning our actions in accord with the new knowledge thus acquired.

Leo Tolstoy

Mystery creates wonder and wonder is the basis of man's desire to understand.

Neil Armstrong

Uncertainty and mystery are energies of life. Don't let them scare you unduly, for they keep boredom at bay and spark creativity.

R. I. Fitzhenry

I would rather live in a world where my life is surrounded by mystery than live in a world so small that my mind could comprehend it.

Harry Emerson Fosdick

All is mystery; but he is a slave who will not struggle to penetrate the dark veil.

Benjamin Disraeli

Coming home

For the first eighteen years of my life, I lived in the same house, on the same street, in the same town. My circle of adventure widened as I grew, from garden to park to town to surrounding areas. But always home was the centre of this circle – the fixed point around which all my other activities whirled.

Then I left home. I travelled for a year, before pitching up in a city to begin my studies. I disliked city life at first – the in-your-face brick walls, the lack of expanse of sky, the permanent neon. But maybe most of all, I hated that it wasn't home. I didn't like being told where to live and having to share it with about four hundred others. I was disconcerted by the many rules and regulations. Living here wasn't like being at home – it felt more like being in a prison.

So I was happy at the end of my first year to move out of my hall of residence into a shared house. But student life was always nomadic. At best you spent a year, maybe two if you were lucky, in the same place with the same housemates. And this nomadic style of existence, moving on from place to place, took root in my mind and set the pattern for the next decade of my life.

Today, jobs and careers seem to make us people on the move. We're the modern pastoralists, moving on to find fruitful pastures. The problem is, unlike our ancestors, we don't take whole communities with us. We travel alone or in ones or twos, and find that where we live isn't so much 'home' as the place we inhabit. We may be surprised to find people who have lived on the same street all their lives.

I myself lived in ten places in the space of ten years, and finally I was tired of moving. I decided the solution was to downsize, to find a place I knew I could afford where I could buy myself some bricks-and-mortar stability – and I went to my hometown to do it.

But why? This was the very town I had been itching to escape from when I was eighteen. Yet after years of being on the move, the idea of being in a place where my family lived, road names were no effort and my memories coincided with the architecture around me, was appealing. I wanted to have a home and to go home.

It's one of the best decisions I've ever made. I love my small, modest house, set in an area of town where people work hard, play hard and know the value of saying 'hello' to their neighbours. Two doors up there's a work-at-home mechanic who services all the cars on the street. Next door, Jaya calls to me across the brick wall that divides our gardens and offers me hot popadoms, while I help her fill out her job application form. The boys on the street congregate to examine snails from the park, compare superhero outfits and bike energetically around the block. I like this sense of strong community. And one of the best things about having a home is the way it releases a new energy in me. Now I'm settled, I have a centre from which I can begin to adventure again.

All this helps me to learn something about the divine. I know in my head that the divine desires each of our hearts as a kind of dwelling place and wants to make a home in us. But what does that mean? Does that mean the divine is restless until it can set up home in us? Maybe. But perhaps more interesting is the idea that the divine can always be at home in us – content, not venturing forwards, but simply being. To know this in our hearts may help make us more relaxed. Wherever we are, we are at home and the divine is at home in us. Our hearts are God's favourite dwelling place on earth. To know this may answer the longing for security that we all carry within us, and create a safe centre from which the adventures of today become a delightful possibility.

Meditation

Read

So he set off and went to his father. But while he was still far off, his father saw him and was filled with compassion; he ran and put his arms around him and kissed him.

Luke 15:20

In my Father's house there are many dwelling-places. If it were not so, would I have told you that I go to prepare a place for you? And if I go and prepare a place for you, I will come again and will take you to myself, so that where I am, there you may be also.

John 14:2–3

Consider

Do you know that the divine cares for you, and that you have a home where you are embraced and kissed with compassion and care?

Can you believe that the divine is at this moment preparing a homecoming for you?

How can you express a sense of home to those who are without a home? Would you like to extend your own sense of belonging to those who lack it?

Imagine

Imagine a child standing at the bottom of a hill, holding onto the handlebars of a bike. The child jumps on the bike and begins to pedal hard. The bike gradually starts to go faster and faster up the hill, the child pedalling all the time. Your attention is drawn to the wheels of the bike. You notice how they turn slowly at first, but, as the bike gains momentum, how they turn more and more quickly. Only the hub of the wheel appears motionless. Soon the child and the bike are both a mass of moving colour and speed. Eventually the child arrives at the top of the hill, applying squealing brakes to come to a breathless standstill. The wheels stop turning and come to a sudden halt.

Imagine that the child represents you at the beginning of the day. Your day starts as you apply energy to turning the wheels of your life. Now think again about the wheels on the bike – how they begin to turn and turn until all is a blur. Could you see that the centre of the wheel, however, was still, even though the spokes of the wheel turned faster and faster? Do you

have a still point around which all the activity of your life turns? If you feel particularly that your life often becomes a rushed, hurried blur, would you like to find a central point to which you can return when needed? How might your home fulfil this function in your life?

Prayer

God of home and homecomings, sometimes there is nothing more you want to do than to shelter us safely. Grant me sanctuary wherever you are pleased to give it. Find a home in my heart as I find a home in yours. Amen.

Poem

Gone fishing

Trout that swim in bright sunshine
Often long for cool, dark shadows.

The fish dream of fronds and weeds
At the riverbank's melting edge.

Just so, sometimes
I wish to be gone, too,

From the glare of noonday brightness,
This certitude of my working day:

I long to enter into a dark mystery,
The sheltering half-sleep of home.

Inspirations

Home is not where you live, but where they understand you.

Christian Morgenstern

Home is a place not only of strong affections, but of entire unreserve. It is life's undress rehearsal, its backroom, its dressing room.

Harriet Beecher Stowe

All that matters is to be at one with the living God
to be a creature in the house of the God of Life.

Like a cat asleep on a chair
at peace, in peace
and at one with the master of the house, with the mistress,
at home, at home in the house of the living,
sleeping on the hearth, and yawning before the fire.

Sleeping on the hearth of the living world
yawning at home before the fire of life
feeling the presence of the living God
like a great reassurance
a deep calm in the heart
a presence
as of the master sitting at the board
in his own and greater being,
in the house of life.

D. H. Lawrence

Where we love is home. Home that our feet may leave, but not our hearts.

Oliver Wendell Holmes

Home is a name, a word. It is a strong one, stronger than any magician ever spoke or spirit ever answered to, in the strongest conjuration.

Charles Dickens

Peace – that was the other name for home.

Kathleen Norris

There is nothing like staying at home for real comfort.

Jane Austen

Home is a place you grow up wanting to leave and grow old wanting to get back to.

John Ed Pearce

Home, the spot of earth supremely blest,
A dearer spot than all the rest.

Robert Montgomery

I had rather be on my farm than be emperor of the world.

George Washington

Home is the one place in all this world where hearts are sure of each other. It is the place of confidence. It is the place where we tear off that mask of guarded and suspicious coldness which the world forces us to wear in self-defence, and where we pour out the unreserved communications of full and confiding hearts. It is the spot where expressions of tenderness gush out without any sensation of awkwardness and without any dread of ridicule.

Frederick W. Robertson

A vision for work

When I look back on my work history, it's the usual pattern of mundane, boring, exciting, stimulating and curious. I'd love to read people's truthful CVs. I don't believe there's any such thing as a straight career path. Me? I've sold flowers from a market stall, filled shelves with baked beans on a supermarket night-shift, been a teacher, photographed people, directed creative teams, acted as a consultant and written just about anything that can be written.

But that's not the whole story of how I fill my time. Work includes all the other ways we spend our time – the essential activities without which life would not function: cleaning, caring for our loved ones, playing with our children, looking after whatever resources we have. That's work, too. I think we have a desperate need to expand our vision of work. It's not simply about what we do to get money in the bank.

Maybe we burn out because our vision of work is too small and not because it's too big. We think all these other activities aren't work and can be squeezed around the edges when our 'real work' allows the time – and this diminished view of 'work' may lead to periods of exhaustion. Or maybe we become disillusioned because, although we are not active in the paid workplace, we are bringing up children or looking after elderly relatives or volunteering in our local community.

Of course, we are not called to do and to be everything. I cannot do well what you do well, even though sometimes our high-achieving culture may lead us to believe that we can all be whatever we want to be, if

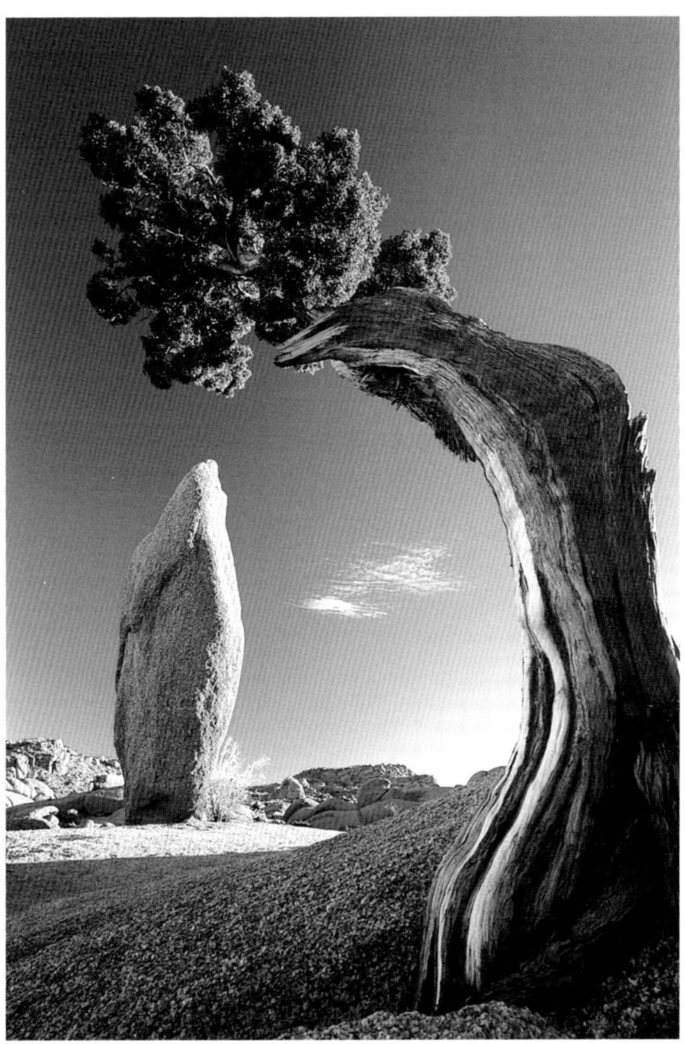

only we'll put in the effort. We may want to develop a more discerning eye for what we are able to do, and to pursue that with vigour.

Part of my sense of work involves drawing a line around what it is I am supposed to be doing. It's not always easy, but when we can discover shapes and patterns and repetitions in our work lives – places where we have had some measure of delight or a sense of exercising something within ourselves – we may want to pay heed to what this is telling us about ourselves and the work to which we are called.

A friend of mine is a teacher and never ceases to be amazed at how her own students, every set of them unique in their mix, manage to teach her new things. Gardeners learn wisdom from their gardens. Scientists stand in awe of the elegance they apprehend in the universal design. Artists contemplate beauty and are themselves transformed by their own contemplations. Parents grow and learn from their own children. And so the list goes on. We give to work and work gives to us – if we are lucky, far more than the figures on a payroll.

That's not to say that work cannot be dehumanizing, intensely stressful and sometimes damaging to us. I have known what it is to work under great pressure and, occasionally, to become ill because of it. But my vision of work seems to grow, rather than to diminish. I find that my sense of what work is and of what we should consider work to be becomes more expanded, more emphatic. My desire to discover and pursue my vocation – in all its scope and all its limitedness – grows.

And the divine is interested in all of it. We can encounter the divine in all the activities of which we are a part. As we do so, we may find that the very work to which we are called and to which we give becomes a giver to us. We shape our work and yet our work, mysteriously, also shapes us.

In all of this, we may like to develop a more patient attitude to ourselves and to our work, for our whole life is a work in which we are invited to collaborate with the divine. In reality, it is the invisible hands of the divine that are moulding us through our work, helping us to become all we are capable of becoming. Our work, however arduous, tedious or time-consuming it may appear at times, is a channel for the divine to be at work in our lives and on our lives. It is a work in which the divine delights.

Meditation

Read

The word that came to Jeremiah from the Lord: 'Come, go down to the potter's house, and there I will let you hear my words.' So I went down to the potter's house, and there he was working at his wheel. The vessel he was making of clay was spoiled in the potter's hand, and he reworked it into another vessel, as seemed good to him. Then the word of the Lord came to me: 'Can I not do with you, O house of Israel, just as this potter has done?' says the Lord. 'Just like the clay in the potter's hand, so are you in my hand, O house of Israel.'

Jeremiah 18:1–6

Or what woman having ten silver coins, if she loses one of them, does not light a lamp, sweep the house, and search carefully until she finds it? When she has found it, she calls together her friends and neighbours, saying, 'Rejoice with me, for I have found the coin that I had lost.' Just so, I tell you, there is joy in the presence of the angels of God over one sinner who repents.'

Luke 15:8–10

To the present hour we are hungry and thirsty, we are poorly clothed and beaten and homeless, and we grow weary from the work of our own hands.

1 Corinthians 4:11–12

For it is God who is at work in you, enabling you both to will and to work for his good pleasure.

Philippians 2:13

For this I toil and struggle with all the energy that he powerfully inspires within me.

Colossians 1:29

Consider

The divine instructs Jeremiah to observe a man at work – a potter – and then makes a profound point to him. Just so, Jesus chooses the example of a woman at work to do the same. Can you believe that the divine is fascinated by human work and that it can become a vehicle of enlightenment and wisdom?

Does your vision of work mean that you will always be successful? Would you say that being hungry, thirsty, poorly clothed, beaten, homeless and weary was an effective example of work? What criteria do you use to judge whether work is worthwhile or not?

Can you believe that your work gives pleasure to the divine? Can you believe that the divine can give you powerful energy with which to toil and struggle?

Imagine

Imagine a mobile phone. It is a useful tool for communicating with others, for reminding yourself of tasks you need to do, for organizing your time, for playing games on, perhaps even to be entertained by. You notice that the bars on your phone's battery are very low. What do you do? Plug it into the charger, perhaps in your car or in your workspace or at home. When it is fully charged, you disconnect the phone and begin to use it again.

Now imagine that you are that mobile phone! You are capable of all these different activities: communicating with, organizing, playing with, even entertaining others. Yet these activities, just like your work, will naturally take energy from you. How do you recharge, even in the middle of work? Can you appreciate that times of recharging directly connect with times of activity and work? Reflect on whether you are getting the right mix of recharging time to do your work effectively – then enjoy the activities of which you are capable.

Prayer

God of activity, you look with interest on all of my work. Work shapes me and I shape it. Thank you that my work can be an expression of my giftedness. I know that this day, this month, this year will not come again. Help me to use my giftedness well in this time. Call me to what you want me to do and help me to do it well. Amen.

Poem

Incantation before work

What are you to make of me?

Set me on fire, O God,
With love and desire
For you and your kingdom.

Light a burning torch in me
That will not go out.

O bless me,

With the benediction of your
Pure and unflinching light.

Inspirations

Some people dream of success, while others wake up and work hard at it.

Anonymous

It is not the long day, but the heart that does the work.

Proverb

A lot of what passes for depression these days is nothing more than a body saying that it needs work.

Geoffrey Norman

Boredom is a sickness, the cure of which is work.

Le Duc de Levis

Work isn't to make more money. You work to justify life.

Marc Chagall

When I work, I relax. Doing nothing or entertaining visitors makes me tired.

Pablo Picasso

Without labour, nothing prospers.

Sophocles

As a cure for worrying, work is better than whisky.

Thomas Edison

We seem as a nation to be suffering from a mania for play. The huge development of pleasure-chasing automobiles merely symbolizes our universal restless eagerness to be running after something, anything, that we can classify as diversion. Under pressure from tormenting constituents, our legislatures are piling up holidays. And the cry of labour everywhere is, 'Cut down hours, cut down hours,' until it seems as if brief, tired minutes were all that would be left for work. The obvious deduction is that work is always something to be got rid of, as if it were a curse. Yet life is work.

Anonymous

Thank God every morning when you get up that you have something to do that day which must be done, whether you like it or not. Being forced to work and forced to do your best will breed in you temperance and self-control, diligence and strength of will, cheerfulness and content and a hundred virtues which the idle never know.

Charles Kingsley

'I worked for men,' my Lord will say, when we meet at the end of the King's highway; 'I walked with the beggar along the road, I kissed the bondsman stung by the goad, I bore my half of the porter's load. And what did you do,' my Lord will say, 'as you travelled along the King's highway?'

Robert Davies

When Earth's last picture is painted, and the tubes are
twisted and dried,
When the oldest colours have faded, and the youngest
critic has died,
We shall rest, and faith, we shall need it – lie down for
an aeon or two,
Till the Master of All Good Workmen shall set us to work
anew.

Rudyard Kipling

The rain of gentleness

My Dad recently received a gift of thanks for forty years' service to the local Volunteer Bureau, whose work involves matching prospective volunteers with charities who need them. The gift was an amateur weather station – perfect for a man who religiously watches the daily weather bulletins, mostly to work out what needs to be done in his beloved garden.

Said weather station consists of a pale grey stake, to be planted in ground 'not too shady, nor too sunny and not near an overhanging wall', (you try finding that spot in the average garden!) and an indoor panel, which gives temperature, wind and precipitation readings. The panel also features a natty digital cartoon figure, who 'dresses' appropriately for the weather.

'Max', as we've dubbed the meteorological digiman, is uncannily accurate. Last week, for example, under balmy blue skies and temperatures nudging the 30s, Max was dressed in a pair of swimming shorts and dark sunglasses. Yet, curiously, he was also holding an unfurled umbrella. Curious, until you consider this is British weather and Max's circumspection is probably understandable.

Despite our high average yearly rainfall, most British weatherpeople describe a drizzly day as 'miserable'. And somehow it's got into our collective psyche: rain equals bad, sun equals good. Yet as I write, the evening sky is turning a dark blue and a light summer rain is beginning to patter on my backyard. I have to come clean: I love the rain.

I love the smell of the rain. I love the feel of it on my skin. I love the sound of the rain. I love the play of water and light, even on grey roads. I love sitting inside, all

cosy, watching the rain fall against the window, and yes, even as an adult, I've played raindrop races.

But maybe I love the rain most of all because it reminds me of gentleness. I'm not talking about torrential rain which reorders whole landscapes, but the gentle rain that comes to refresh the earth. In this way gentleness and refreshment, at least in my mind, become linked.

Every time I hear the rain (which is frequent), I try to remember the joy and blessing of gentleness, and that such gentleness can refresh me and others, just as the blessing of rain refreshes the thirsty earth. Furthermore, I remember that the divine is often gentle with me and that such encounters make me sigh with relief, just as my summer plants seem to sigh with thanks when the first raindrops begin to fall.

I think we all want to be touched gently. We all want to be spoken to gently. We all want, at times, to be held lightly. Further, we can discover the joy of touching others, speaking to others, holding others gently. And we realize the joy of being gentle with ourselves. We may begin to love the refreshment that this brings.

Meditation

Read

'Give ear, O heavens, and I will speak; let the earth hear the words of my mouth. May my teaching drop as the rain, my speech distil as the dew, as the gentle rain upon the tender grass, and as the showers upon the herb.'

Deuteronomy 32:1–2

But the wisdom from above is first pure, then peaceable, gentle, open to reason, full of mercy and good fruits, without uncertainty or insincerity.

James 3:17

But we were gentle among you, like a nurse taking care of her children. So, being affectionately desirous of you, we were ready to share with you not only the gospel of God but also our own selves, because you had become very dear to us. For you remember our labor and toil, brethren; we worked night and day, that we might not burden any of you, while we preached to you the gospel of God. You are witnesses, and God also, how holy and righteous and blameless was our behavior to you believers.

1 Thessalonians 2:7-10

Take my yoke upon you, and learn from me; for I am gentle and humble in heart, and you will find rest for your souls.

Matthew 11:29

Consider

Would you like your speech to be gentle today? What difference might it make to your message and to your hearers for you to speak gently, even though you may have difficult things to say?

Which words would you use to describe wisdom? Is 'gentle' on your list?

If you exercise a position of leadership, how do you feel towards those who are in your care? Is gentleness an important part of your style? Do you encourage gentleness – without promoting bad behaviour – in your workplace culture?

Jesus' words imply that the divine values a gentle heart. Yet maybe your gentle heart has been bruised by aggressive encounters. Can you let God heal your bruises?

Imagine

It is dusk in a garden. You are watching a woman approach her lover in this beautiful garden. She walks slowly up the garden path to where her lover is waiting. The air is full of the scent of fragrant plants. The sky is turning a light blue. There is a soft breeze. There is no urgency in the way the woman moves. She walks gently and unhurriedly. Finally she reaches her lover's arms and they gently embrace. They whisper softly to each other, 'You are mine and you belong to me.'

In this meditation, were you the woman or the waiting lover? How does it feel to know that there is no need for urgency in your life? Can you see that anticipation, trust and waiting are all parts of gentleness, too? And that these can be blessed, joyful and beautiful things? The divine does not hurry you, but is always gentle. Maybe you need to hear the gentle words of love and belonging that the divine lover whispers to you today.

Prayer

God of tenderness and gentleness, I eat, sleep, work, rest and play in you. Feed me with your love. Strengthen me with your peace. Rest me with your care. Caress me with your gentle spirit. Help me to know that there is no urgency with you. Amen.

Poem

A gentle season

Breath of summer rain,
Cool waves,
Fleece on the beach,
My child's warm hand in mine.

Inspirations

Nothing feebler does earth nurture than man,
Of all things living and breathing.

Homer

Always be a little kinder than necessary.

J. M. Barrie

How beautiful a day can be when kindness touches it!

George Elliston

Gentleness does more than violence.

French proverb

Patience and gentleness is power.

Leigh Hunt

I learned that it is the weak who are cruel, and that gentleness is to be expected only from the strong.

Leo Rosten

Nothing is so strong as gentleness and nothing is so gentle as real strength.

Ralph W. Sockman

A gentle hand may lead even an elephant by a hair.

Proverb

Jesus, as a mother you gather your people to you: you are gentle with us as a mother with her children; often you weep over our sins and our pride: tenderly you draw us from hatred and judgement. You comfort us in sorrow and bind up our wounds: in sickness you nurse us, and with pure milk you feed us. Jesus, by your dying we are born to new life: by your anguish and labour we come forth in joy. Despair turns to hope through your sweet goodness: through your gentleness we find comfort in fear.

Anselm of Canterbury

Too often we underestimate the power of a touch, a smile, a kind word, a listening ear, an honest compliment or the smallest act of caring, all of which would have the potential to turn a life around.

Leo Buscaglia

The more thou dam'st it up, the more it
burns.
The current that with gentle murmur
glides,
Thou know'st, being stopped,
impatiently doth rage;
But when his fair course is not
hindered,
He makes sweet music with th'
enameled stones,
Giving a gentle kiss to every sedge,
He overtaketh in his pilgrimage.
And so by many winding nooks he
strays
With willing sport to the wild ocean.
Then let me go and hinder not my
course.
I'll be as patient as a gentle stream
And make a pastime of each weary
step,
Till the last step have brought me to
my love;
And there I'll rest, as after much turmoil
A blessed soul doth in Elysium.

William Shakespeare

A bit of fragrance always clings to the hand that gives roses.

Chinese proverb

We do not very often come across opportunities for exercising strength, magnanimity, or magnificence; but gentleness, temperance, modesty, and humility, are graces which ought to colour everything we do.

François de Sales

Making our peace

I was idly flicking through an old journal of mine when I came across an entry entitled: 'We are all made for peace.' In it, I had detailed a visit I'd made to a refugee family now living in the UK.

Ben and Kongosi Mussanzi had been forced to flee their beloved homeland, the Democratic Republic of Congo, due to the violent fighting which to date has claimed over four million lives. Ben had related to me how he himself had been threatened while on the way to celebrate a family wedding. A gang of drugged-up teenage militia had spent time discussing in front of him how they were going to murder him. By the grace of God, he says, he was spared.

Deeply shaken by the incident, Ben vowed to help bring an end to the violence in his country in whatever way he could. He and his wife eventually set up a centre of conflict resolution. But the work was far from easy and was not without its risks.

Later, Ben came to the UK to do a PhD in peace studies, but violence at home intensified and Kongosi and his four children were forced to hide out in the African bush for a month, before being taken to safety and finally granted asylum in the UK. Other members of staff at the conflict resolution centre were murdered (as documented by Amnesty International).

Despite the trauma, heartache and anxiety of their personal lives, Ben and Kongosi's desire for peacemaking has not waned. Despite their love for their country, they know it would be suicide to return and so have decided to concentrate on peacemaking initiatives in the country which, they gratefully acknowledge, has given them hospitality and temporary shelter. Eventually they hope to return home and found a Pan African University, which will specifically study issues of conflict and peace.

Ben and Kongosi's story, though heart-wrenching, is not unique. All around our world countless conflicts rage – some we know about and some we rarely, if ever, glimpse. Yet conflict occurs not only on an international stage, but in our own communities, workplaces and families.

I have faced the threat of violence several times in my own life. I have known what it is to be in intensely insecure situations. I have even faced what it means to know that someone wants to kill you. Thankfully, for me such incidences were short-lived, but their impact can be lasting. What I have learned is that what the violent try to destroy, the divine comes to heal and to restore.

Part of that healing and restoration comes through peace. The divine is passionately interested in and committed to peace – for continents, countries, cities, towns and villages; between neighbours, between friends, in families and yes, even within ourselves. The divine desires that great peace rests in us – in mind, heart, body, soul and spirit.

And what are the tools of the peacemaker in our outer world today? I would suggest these: forgiveness instead of hatred, gentleness in the face of violence, faith instead of fear, blessing instead of cursing, compassion in the place of condemnation. We all at some stage in our lives face situations of conflict, whether we live in a country that is overtly unstable or not. How will we respond? Peacemaking may be part of our vocation.

Yet peacemaking is arduous work. As aspiring peacemakers, we need to embrace rhythm and balance in our lives. We need to allow ourselves the replenishing graces of play, recreation, meditation, rest, friendship and sleep, for example. We cannot bear the burden of every conflict around the world – nor are we meant to. The divine knows how to oppose violence and we can draw on the tenderness of the divine counsel. As peacemakers,

we can work with our eyes on those of the One who is the ultimate maker of Peace, who perfectly loves us and always desires our well-being.

Meditation

Read

Look, I am going to send peace flowing over her like a river.

Isaiah 66:12

They have treated the wound of my people carelessly, saying, 'Peace, peace,' when there is no peace.

Jeremiah 6:14

Blessed are the peacemakers, for they will be called children of God.

Matthew 5:9

Consider

Can you think of people, situations or countries where you would like to see peace flowing like a river? Or maybe you need peace to flow over you like a river? Name the focus of your current desire for peace.

Do you believe that the divine is passionately interested in and deeply committed to peace? If you want to compose a lament about violence, can you express it? Can you believe the divine might feel the same way?

If you have a desire for peace, can you see that this desire may itself originate from the divine heart? Can you believe that the divine will help you to be a peacemaker and that in your work as a peacemaker, however large or small, you demonstrate your own kinship with the divine?

Imagine

Imagine that you are standing on the edge of a large white sailboat, which is anchored in a calm, turquoise sea. You have a snorkel, flippers and a mask and are being invited to jump into the clear waters. You do so. You swim through the clear waters for some minutes, noticing the way the light filters through the clear water to the sandy seabed below. Suddenly you come upon a coral reef. It is vibrant with colour, and all kinds of fish are darting in and out of it. You feel as though you are swimming in an aquarium. You notice small shoals of brightly coloured fish chasing each other; sea anemones, even flatfish puffing up the sand on the floor of the seabed. You stay for as long as you wish.

How did you feel when you contemplated jumping off the side of the boat into the waters? What did you expect to see when you got into the water? What was it like when you were paddling through the clear waters and then suddenly came upon the sight of the coral reef, alive with all kinds of aquatic life? What did it feel like to know that you could stay for as long as you liked on the coral reef? Did you have any other emotions as you were there?

Can you imagine peace as the clear waters into which you jumped? Can you see that peace may yield up all sorts of surprising life to you – just as the calm waters in your meditation were home to the life of the coral reef? What surprises or delights would you like to find in your own experiences of peace? How might peace nurture life in the situations you are facing today?

Prayer

God of peace and life, I want to jump into your peace. I know that I need your presence before I can be a peacemaker in your world. Fill me with your peace, so that I overflow with it. Heal any fears or anxieties I have. May I experience your life-giving peace and bring its power to situations and people today. Amen.

Poem

Circles of dreams

I napped
That buttermilk sunset,

Bare feet flung casually
Over the edge of a chair,

Breathing deeply, unknowingly
Caressed
By the sigh of a cool breeze.

O Peace,

When I weary of your work
In the world today,

Receive me.

Let me lie down with you
And dream
Whole circles of dreams.

Inspirations

Where there is peace, God is.
George Herbert

A late lark twitters from the quiet skies:
And from the west,
Where the sun, his day's work ended,
Lingers as in content,
There falls on the old, gray city
An influence luminous and serene,
A shining peace.
William Ernest Henley

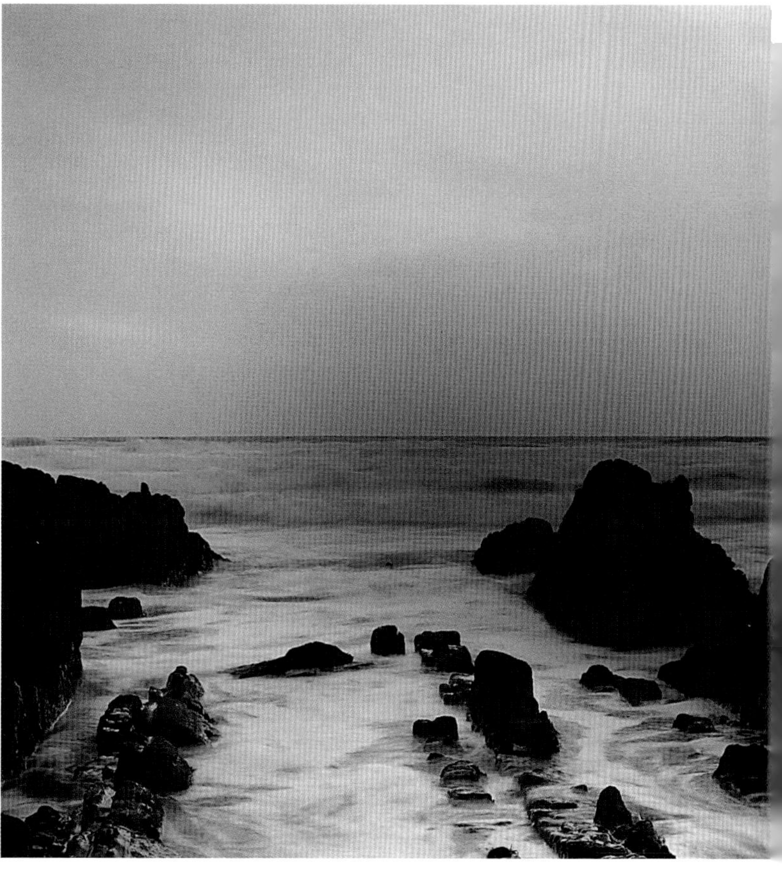

The fiercest agonies have shortest reign;
And after dreams of horror, comes again
The welcome morning with its rays of peace.

William Cullen Bryant

Press bravely onward! – not in vain
Your generous trust in human kind;
The good which bloodshed could not gain
Your peaceful zeal shall find.

John Greenleaf Whittier

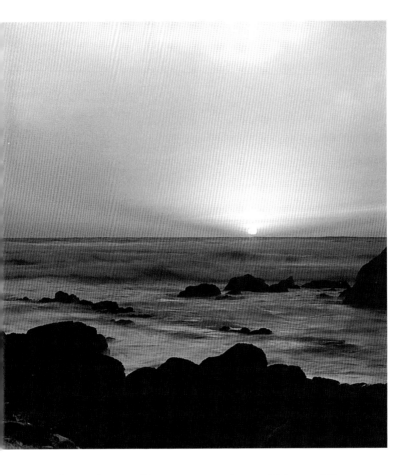

All His glory and beauty come from within, and there He delights to dwell. His visits there are frequent, His conversation sweet, His comforts refreshing; and His peace passing all understanding.

Thomas à Kempis

If there is beauty in character, there will be harmony in the home. If there is harmony in the home, there will be order in the nation. If there is order in the nation, there will be peace in the world.

Proverb

Peace and tranquillity are a thousand gold pieces.

Proverb

Soft peace she brings, wherever she arrives:
She builds our quiet, as she forms our lives:
Lays the rough paths of peevish Nature even,
And opens in each heart a little Heaven.

Matthew Prior

Peace hath her victories
No less renown'd than war.

John Milton

Peace has no borders.

Yitzhak Rabin

Peace is rarely denied to the peaceful.

Friedrich von Schiller

Peace is the gift of God. Do you want peace? Go to God. Do you want peace in your families? Go to God. Do you want peace to brood over your families? If you do, live your religion, and the very peace of God will dwell and abide with you, for that is where peace comes from, and it doesn't dwell anywhere else.

John Taylor

The gift of ourselves

I was standing in a long queue at my local supermarket. Tired and bored, I shifted my weight from one foot to the other. In my left hand, I was clutching a beige bucket for a floor mop. Currently the bucket held nothing more romantic than toilet cleaner, a box of washing powder and a white bowl. In my right hand, I grasped an A2 layout pad and a pack of pens, which held the promise of infinitely more exciting possibilities, because I needed the pad and pens for some creative work.

As I stood there, half bored, half daydreaming, it struck me how accurate a snapshot of life this was. Here I was, prosaic toilet cleaner in one hand, while in the other were the tools of a fiery creativity I love. It seemed strangely symbolic somehow. A mix of the mundane and the marvellous. All our lives, I further reflected, are full of the ordinary and full of this kind of glory.

With nothing so familiar as our hands, we wipe up, we eat, we touch a child's face in love, we grasp a hurting friend. With these same hands, we write shopping lists and we write sonnets. Our ordinary selves are capable of the small details of life and the great adventures, too.

Yes, our beautiful bodies succumb to the ravages of disease and decay, if not to deep weariness. Our minds may be darkened or confused. Our hearts may be hurt. Yet we may also run and dance with great energy and wild abandon. Our minds may grasp and solve complex questions, offering up radical and life-changing solutions. Our hearts heal and love again. Always, there is this pattern of light, dark, light, dark.

Just so, we have days when we struggle through a fog of doubt, half-heartedness and lethargy. On other days, we may know a kind of ecstasy of the soul, where we walk and leap our lives in bright conviction. We stretch to live at white heat, our hearts expanded, but we are not always successful. In this way, we rise and fall like waves on the ocean. And we come to discover what it means to live with passion and purpose, as well as to accept the lulls. Even in the mix, we are blessed.

Yet sooner or later, we may find there is no other place that can hold the expanse of our wild hearts than the hands of the infinite divine. But it may be just these hands – these tender, cherishing hands – that break us. Breaking may come in the experiences of hardship, grief, difficulty, challenge and stress. These are not enemies to our vocation as the beloved – and may, in fact, be strangers who help us travel more deeply into our authentic journey of love and being loved.

So we should not be unduly alarmed if our days are not all ones of ease and comfort. On the contrary, our path through life may bring us difficult experiences. These experiences do not and should not negate our sense of worth. If these experiences come by divine provenance, we can be sure that the breaking is for a purpose. So why are our beautiful, blessed selves broken? I believe we are broken, as a loaf of bread is broken between two hands, so that we can be given.

And this is the final truth: we are all gifts, you and I. We are each and every one of us, literally, God's gift to the world. In our mundanity and doubt, no less than in our glory and conviction, we are gifts – as our feet stand in the mud, even while we contemplate the stars.

Meditation

Read

For it is the God who said, 'Let light shine out of darkness,' who has shone in our hearts to give the light of the knowledge of the glory of God in the face of Jesus Christ. But we have this treasure in clay jars, so that it may be made clear that this extraordinary power belongs to God and does not come from us.

2 Corinthians 4:6–7

And all of us, with unveiled faces, seeing the glory of the Lord as though reflected in a mirror, are being transformed into the same image from one degree of glory to another; for this comes from the Lord, the Spirit.

2 Corinthians 3:18

I will give a white stone, and on the white stone is written a new name that no one knows except the one who receives it.

Revelation 2:17

Consider

How can you see and honour the giftedness in yourself today? How can you see and honour the giftedness in others around you? (For example, practise an aspect of your own giftedness, offer a word or smile of encouragement to others or give thanks for your own or another's giftedness.)

Do you experience both a bright sense of faith or conviction and also a sense of your own humanity or frailty? Does this surprise you or do you accept it?

Do you have a sense of your own ongoing transformation? What name might be written on your unique white stone?

Imagine

Imagine that you are looking at a life-size photo of yourself dressed from head to foot in white. In your hand you hold a great, fat, black marker pen. You are being invited to write over yourself who you really think you are, the attributes of yourself that are most important and most authentic to you, whether they currently have daily expression or not. Write those names over the photo – for example, carer, parent, friend, artist, engineer, teacher, drifter, poet, counsellor or musician.

When you have finished your meditation, you may like to write down some of the words you chose to describe who you really are. Perhaps you would like to think about ways of bringing yourself deliberately as that person to God. When you are truly yourself, you may find that God is very close.

Prayer

God of my heart, return me to myself, that my whole self may praise you, that my whole life may be a song and a dance for you. Let me stand before you with confidence and say, 'Yes, this is how you made me. How good you are.' Amen.

Poem

Gift of one

I brought him old gold
From distant rivers,
But beneath that star,
We found strange kingdom treasure:

A baby, fresh minted,
New currency of love.

Inspirations

Our hearts are restless until they come to rest in Thee.

St Augustine

Our birth is but a sleep and a forgetting
The soul that rises with us, our life's star
Hath had elsewhere its setting
And cometh from afar:
Not in entire forgetfulness,
And not in utter nakedness
But trailing clouds of glory do we come
From God who is our home.

William Wordsworth

The most gifted members of the human species are at their creative best when they cannot have their way, and must compensate for what they miss by realizing and cultivating their capacities and talents.

Eric Hoffer

I am climbing a difficult road; but the glory gives me strength.

Sextus Propertius

Endurance is not just the ability to bear a hard thing, but to turn it into glory.

William Barclay

Glory is never where virtue is not.

Martin le Franc

Glory follows virtue as if it were its shadow.

Cicero

Unless what we do is useful, our glory is vain.

Phaedrus

The glory of God is a living man; and the life of man consists in beholding God.

Irenaeus

Text Acknowledgments

pp. 14–15 Scripture quotations are from The Holy Bible, English Standard Version, published by HarperCollins Publishers, copyright © 2001 Crossway Bibles, a division of Good News Publishers. Used by permission. All rights reserved.

p. 18 Extract from 'Debt' by Jessie B Rittenhouse. Reprinted by permission of the Department of College Archives and Special Collections, Olin Library, Rollins College, Winter Park, Florida.

pp. 15, 22, 28, 37, 44, 45, 53, 60, 68, 74, 82, 91, 99, 106, 114, 123–124 Scripture quotations taken from the Revised Standard Version/New Revised Standard Version published by HarperCollins Publishers, copyright © 1989 by the Division of Christian Education of the National Council of the Churches of Christ in the USA, and are used by permission. All rights reserved.

pp. 29, 107, 114 Scripture quotations taken from the Holy Bible, New International Version, copyright © 1973, 1978, 1984 International Bible Society. Used by permission of Zondervan and Hodder & Stoughton Limited. All rights reserved. The 'NIV' and 'New International Version' trademarks are registered in the United States Patent and Trademark Office by International Bible Society. Use of either trademark requires the permission of International Bible Society. UK trademark number 1448790.

pp. 37 Taken from the New Jerusalem Bible, published and copyright © 1985 by Darton, Longman and Todd Ltd and les Editions du Cerf, and by Doubleday, a division of Bantam Doubleday Dell Publishing Group, Inc. Used by permission of Darton, Longman and Todd Ltd, and Doubleday, a division of Random House, Inc.

p. 60 Scripture quotation is from the Good News Bible published by The Bible Societies/HarperCollins Publishers, copyright © 1966, 1971, 1976, 1992 American Bible Society.

p. 68 Scripture quotation is taken from the Holy Bible, New Living Translation, copyright © 1996. Used by permission of Tyndale House Publishers, Inc., Wheaton, Illinois 60189. All rights reserved.

p. 103 Extract from 'When Earth's Last Picture is Painted' by Rudyard Kipling. Reprinted by permission of A P Watts Ltd on behalf of The National Trust for Places of Historic Interest or Natural Beauty.